ZERMATT T

GUIDE 2025

Expert Guide to the Best Hiking Experience, Scenic Drives, Skiing, History, Culture, and is Full of Colored Images and Maps Appropriate for First-Time Visitors.

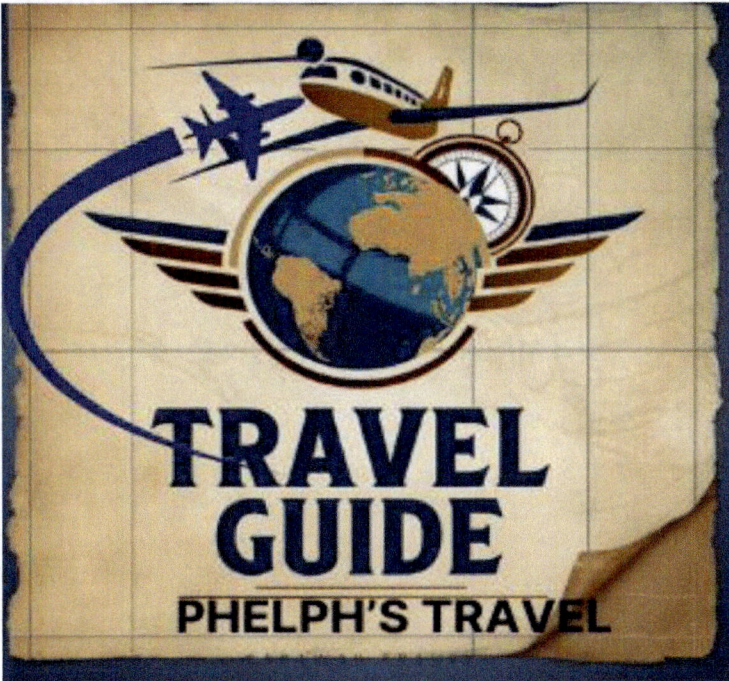

Johnny A. Phelps

Disclaimer

The information contained in this Zermatt Travel Guide 2025 is intended to be used for informational purposes only. The author, Johnny A. Phelps, has made every effort to ensure that the information provided is accurate and up-to-date at the time of publication. However, it is important to note that conditions in the Zermatt region can change rapidly, and the information contained in this guide may not reflect the most current situation.

The recommendations, suggestions, and advice provided in this guide are based on the author's personal experiences and extensive research. While the author has taken great care to ensure the accuracy and reliability of the information, readers should always verify the current conditions, regulations, and safety protocols with local authorities, tourism offices, or other official sources before embarking on their Zermatt adventure.

Outdoor activities, such as hiking, skiing, and mountaineering, carry inherent risks. Readers are advised to exercise caution, obtain proper training and equipment, and consult with experienced local guides when engaging in these pursuits. The author and publisher cannot be held responsible for any injuries, accidents, or damages that may occur during a reader's visit to Zermatt.

This guide is not intended to replace professional medical advice, legal counsel, or financial planning. Readers are encouraged to seek appropriate expertise in these areas as needed.

The author and publisher make no warranties, expressed or implied, regarding the information contained in this travel guide and shall not be liable for any errors, omissions, or damages arising from its use. By using this Zermatt Travel Guide 2025, readers acknowledge and agree to these disclaimers and limitations of liability.

Contents

CHAPTER 1.

INTRODUCTION TO ZERMATT

Welcome to Zermatt - A Jewel in the Swiss Alps

Nestled in the heart of the Swiss Alps, at the foot of the iconic Matterhorn, lies the picturesque village of Zermatt - a true alpine gem that has captured the imagination of travelers from around the world. Situated at an elevation of 1,620 meters (5,310 feet) in the canton of Valais, Zermatt is a world-renowned destination celebrated for its breathtaking natural beauty, rich history, and unparalleled outdoor adventures.

This car-free alpine oasis, which has a permanent population of slightly more than 5,800 people, is widely regarded as one of the most beautiful and well-preserved mountain communities in the Alps. Surrounded by a stunning glacial landscape and towering, snow-capped peaks, Zermatt is in a privileged position in the Pennine Alps, offering visitors a truly immersive and awe-inspiring experience of Switzerland's majestic alpine wonderland.

The iconic Matterhorn

The Matterhorn is Zermatt's most famous natural landmark and, arguably, one of the world's most recognizable mountains. Standing at 4,478 meters (14,692 feet), this iconic peak, with its distinctive pyramidal shape, has captivated mountaineers, adventurers, and tourists for generations. The first successful ascent of the Matterhorn in 1865 was a watershed moment in alpinism history, and it is still a sought-after challenge for the world's most experienced climbers.

A Rich History and Cultural Heritage

Zermatt's origins can be traced back to the 13th century, when the village first emerged as a small agricultural and pastoral settlement. Over the centuries, Zermatt grew into an important trading post and regional transportation hub, eventually becoming a world-class alpine resort in the nineteenth century. Throughout its long history, the village has maintained a strong cultural identity, with traditional Swiss architecture, time-honored customs, and a thriving artisanal community all contributing to its distinct sense of place.

A year-round destination.

Zermatt is a true four-season destination, with an exceptional range of activities and experiences to delight visitors at all times of the year. In the winter, the village transforms into a premier ski and snowboard destination, with more than 360 kilometers of groomed pistes, cutting-edge lift systems, and some of Europe's highest ski areas. During the warmer months, Zermatt shines as a destination for hikers, climbers, mountain bikers, and anyone looking to immerse themselves in the beauty of the Swiss Alps.

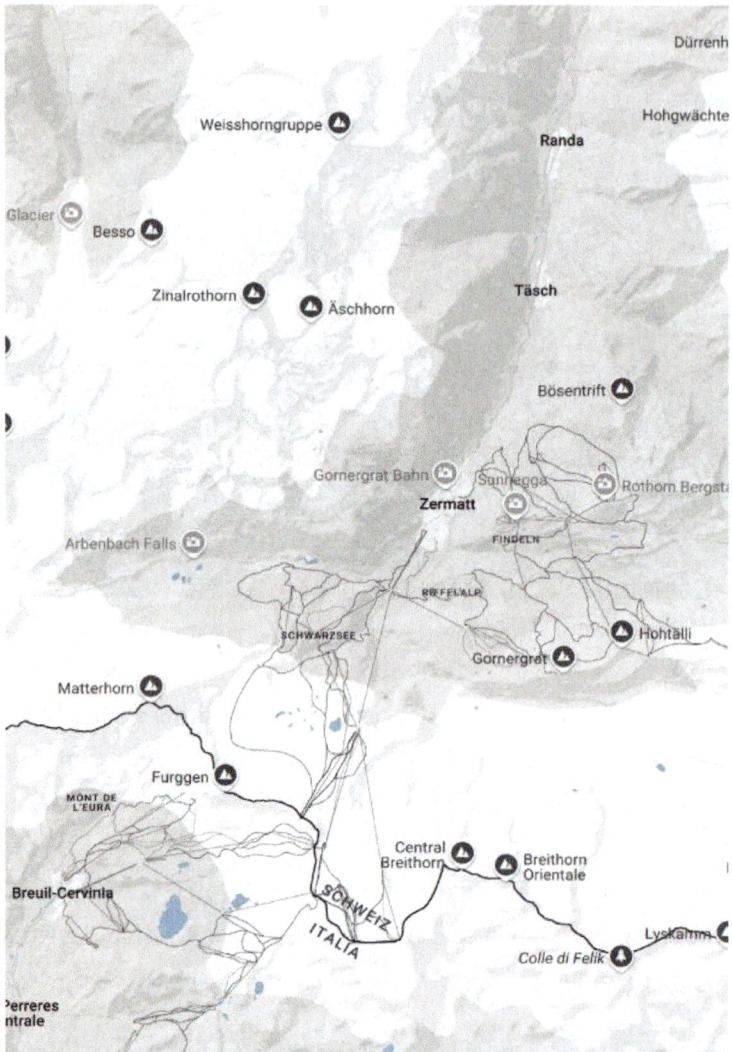

Whether you're drawn to Zermatt for its rich cultural heritage, world-class outdoor activities, or simply to take in the breathtaking natural scenery, this enchanting alpine village will leave an indelible impression. As you prepare for your Zermatt adventure, let this comprehensive travel guide be your trusted companion, revealing the best of this truly exceptional Swiss destination.

Brief History and Cultural Heritage

Zermatt's history is deeply intertwined with the story of the Swiss Alps, stretching back centuries and brimming with tales of adventurous mountain explorations, resilient alpine communities, and the enduring allure of this magnificent corner of the world.

The earliest recorded mention of Zermatt dates back to the 13th century, when the village began to emerge as a small agricultural and pastoral settlement populated by hardy mountain dwellers. These early inhabitants subsisted on livestock farming, cheese production, and the harvesting of resources from the surrounding forests and meadows – a way of life that would come to define the village's cultural identity for generations to come.

Zermatt's strategic location along important trade and transportation routes transformed it into a regional commercial hub over the centuries. The arrival of the Simplon Pass in the early nineteenth century, which connected the village to Italy, increased Zermatt's economic importance by making it an essential stopover point for merchants, pilgrims, and adventurers traveling through the rugged alpine terrain.

During this period of increased activity and exposure, Zermatt began to capture the attention of the wider world. The first successful ascent of the Matterhorn in 1865 by a team led by Edward Whymper shook the international mountaineering community, cementing the village's reputation as a top destination for alpinists and adventurers. This pivotal event, marked by both triumph and tragedy, would shape Zermatt's reputation as a hub of alpine exploration and innovation.

As the nineteenth century came to an end, Zermatt underwent a remarkable transformation, from a remote agricultural outpost to a thriving alpine resort catering to an increasing influx of tourists and leisure travelers. The construction of the Gornergrat Railway, one of Europe's highest rack railways, in 1898 was a watershed moment, providing visitors with unparalleled access to the Pennine Alps' breathtaking scenery. This new era saw a surge in hotel construction, the development of winter sports facilities, and the preservation of Zermatt's distinctive architectural heritage, all of which contributed to the village's reputation as a world-class alpine destination.

Today, Zermatt proudly embraces its rich history while blending tradition and modernity. The village's historic center, complete with charming wooden chalets, narrow cobblestone streets, and the iconic church steeple, exemplifies the community's enduring cultural identity. Meanwhile, the presence of cutting-edge ski infrastructure, innovative dining establishments, and a vibrant community of artisans and creatives keeps Zermatt at the forefront of alpine tourism and innovation.

Throughout its history, Zermatt has held a deep respect for the natural world around it. The village's car-free policy, dedication to sustainable development, and numerous opportunities for immersive outdoor experiences all demonstrate a deep respect for the fragile alpine ecosystem. The harmonious coexistence of human settlement and breathtaking natural landscape is perhaps Zermatt's most distinguishing feature, making it a truly exceptional and inspiring destination.

As you wander the streets of this captivating alpine village, you'll be struck by the palpable sense of history, tradition, and the enduring human spirit that permeates every corner. From the iconic Matterhorn to the charming wooden chalets, Zermatt's cultural heritage is woven into the very fabric of the place, offering visitors a truly immersive and authentic Swiss alpine experience.

Seasons and Best Times to Visit

As a world-class alpine destination, Zermatt offers an exceptional year-round experience, with each season presenting its own unique charms and attractions. Whether you're seeking a thrilling winter wonderland, a rejuvenating summer retreat, or a vibrant shoulder season adventure, Zermatt is poised to deliver an unforgettable visit tailored to your preferences.

Winter in Zermatt

The winter months, from December to April, are unquestionably the most popular time to visit Zermatt, as the village transforms into a top ski and snowboard destination. During this magical season, the surrounding peaks are blanketed in pristine, powdery white, offering downhill enthusiasts unparalleled opportunities. Zermatt's ski areas, which include the Matterhorn Glacier Paradise and the Gornergrat region, offer over 360 kilometers of meticulously groomed pistes served by a cutting-edge network of lifts and cable cars. Thrill-seekers can take on challenging runs, while those who prefer a slower pace can enjoy scenic cross-country ski trails and winter hikes.

Beyond the slopes, Zermatt provides a plethora of winter activities to entice visitors. Enjoy the village's well-known après-ski scene, which includes traditional Swiss raclette and fondue as well as live entertainment. Adventurers can go on guided snowshoeing expeditions, visit the enchanting Igloo Village, or even try their hand at curling. The winter months also bring a slew of cultural events and festivals to Zermatt, including the vibrant Zermatt Unplugged music festival and the enchanting Christmas markets.

The best time to visit Zermatt in winter is usually from January to March, when snow conditions are at their best and the village is bustling with activity. However, it is important to note that the peak holiday season, especially around Christmas and New Year's, can be the busiest and most expensive time to visit. If your schedule is flexible, consider booking your winter vacation in early

December or late April to avoid crowds and possibly lower lodging rates.

Summer in Zermatt.

While Zermatt is well-known for its world-class winter sports, the summer months provide a delightful and equally compelling experience. From June to September, the surrounding alpine meadows bloom with vibrant wildflowers, and the snowcapped peaks serve as a breathtaking backdrop for a variety of outdoor activities.

Hiking enthusiasts will be in their element, with over 400 kilometers of well-marked trails ranging from leisurely valley strolls to strenuous climbs. Explore the picturesque Gorner Gorge, hike to the iconic Matterhorn Glacier, or embark on a multi-day trekking adventure through the breathtaking Pennine Alps. For a unique perspective, take a scenic ride on the Gornergrat Bahn, which takes passengers to Europe's highest open-air railway station at 3,089 meters.

Beyond hiking, Zermatt has a plethora of summer activities to entice visitors. Thrill-seekers can go rock climbing, mountain biking, and even glacier trekking, while those who prefer a slower pace can go standup paddleboarding on the pristine lakes or simply relax in the village's charming cafes and squares. The summer months also bring a thriving cultural calendar to Zermatt, with festivals, concerts, and art exhibitions celebrating the region's rich history.

The best time to visit Zermatt in the summer is usually between mid-June and August, when the weather is warmest and the days are longest. However, keep in mind that this is also peak tourist season, which means higher hotel rates and potentially larger crowds. If you want a more relaxing experience, plan your summer visit for late spring (May) or early autumn (September), when the weather is still mild and the village is less crowded.

Shoulder Season in Zermatt

The shoulder seasons of spring (April-May) and autumn (October-November) provide a delightful alternative for those looking to explore Zermatt at a slower pace. During these transitional periods, the village has a quieter, more peaceful atmosphere, with fewer tourists and often less expensive lodging options.

Zermatt comes alive in the spring as the winter snow slowly melts, revealing vibrant alpine meadows and the first signs of new life. This is an ideal time to explore the village's hiking trails and witness the dramatic transformation of the landscape. Autumn, on the other hand, brings a spectacular display of fall foliage, with the surrounding forests and mountainsides erupting in a tapestry of warm colors. This is an ideal time for leisurely strolls, photography, and indulging in the village's outstanding culinary offerings.

Regardless of the season, it's important to remember that Zermatt's high-altitude location means that the weather is unpredictable and conditions can change quickly. It's always a good idea to bring layers, sturdy footwear, and be prepared for unexpected temperature and precipitation changes. Checking the forecast and remaining flexible with your itinerary can help you make the most of your Zermatt experience, regardless of when you visit.

10 Reasons Why Zermatt Should Be on Your Bucket List

Nestled in the heart of the Swiss Alps, the picturesque village of Zermatt is a true alpine gem that should be on every traveler's bucket list. From its breathtaking natural landscapes to its rich cultural heritage and diverse array of outdoor adventures, Zermatt offers an unparalleled experience that captivates visitors from around the world. Here are ten compelling reasons why you should add this Swiss alpine wonder to your must-visit destinations:

The Iconic Matterhorn: Undoubtedly Zermatt's most recognizable landmark, the Matterhorn is a true icon of the Swiss Alps. This majestic, pyramid-shaped peak stands tall at 4,478 meters (14,692 feet), inspiring awe and respect in all who see it. Whether you admire it from the village or go on a thrilling mountaineering expedition, the Matterhorn is a sight that will leave an impression.

Breathtaking Glacial Landscapes: The Zermatt region is home to a number of impressive glaciers, including the Gorner, Findel, and Theodul glaciers. These massive ice rivers carve their way through the alpine terrain, revealing stunning vistas and providing insight into the region's geological history. Visitors can explore these glacial wonders on guided tours or take a scenic helicopter ride for a bird's-eye perspective.

Unrivalled Hiking and Trekking: With over 400 kilometers (250 miles) of well-marked hiking trails, Zermatt provides countless opportunities for outdoor enthusiasts to immerse themselves in the region's natural beauty. The area welcomes hikers of all skill levels, from gentle strolls through alpine meadows to challenging multi-day treks. Experienced guides can take you on memorable excursions while sharing their knowledge of the local flora, fauna, and geological formations.

World-Class Skiing and Snowboarding: Zermatt's high-altitude slopes and glaciers make it a top choice for winter sports enthusiasts. The resort's interconnected ski areas, including Gornergrat and Matterhorn Glacier Paradise, provide exceptional skiing and snowboarding opportunities, complete with well-groomed pistes, challenging off-piste runs, and breathtaking views of the Matterhorn. The town's ski infrastructure, which includes modern lifts and cutting-edge snowmaking technology, ensures a consistent and enjoyable winter sports season.

Vibrant Cultural Heritage: Zermatt has a rich cultural heritage that is deeply rooted in Alpine traditions and history. Visitors can explore the charming old town, which features distinctive wooden chalets and narrow streets, as well as learn about local customs and crafts. From traditional cheese-making demonstrations to musical performances, Zermatt reveals the Swiss mountain people's enduring spirit and resilience.

Diverse Dining and Culinary Delights: As a well-known alpine destination, Zermatt takes pride in its culinary offerings. The town has a diverse range of restaurants, from cozy mountain huts serving hearty Swiss fare to Michelin-starred establishments highlighting the region's best ingredients. Foodies can enjoy local specialties such as raclette, fondue, and Swiss-style rösti, as well as explore the lively après-ski scene and sample the region's renowned wines and spirits.

Unrivalled Aerial Sightseeing: For a truly breathtaking view of the Swiss Alps, consider booking a scenic helicopter tour over Zermatt and the surrounding area. These exhilarating excursions provide unobstructed views of the Matterhorn, the Gorner Glacier, and other breathtaking peaks and valleys, making for an unforgettable experience. Just keep any vertigo or motion sickness concerns in mind, and if you're feeling adventurous, book a "doors-off" flight.

Wellness and Relaxation: Following a day of outdoor adventures, Zermatt provides numerous opportunities to unwind and recharge. Many of the town's hotels and spas offer cutting-edge wellness facilities, such as indoor and outdoor pools, saunas, and rejuvenating treatments. Visitors can enjoy a luxurious massage, soak in a hot tub with panoramic views, or simply relax in the peaceful alpine setting, allowing the stresses of daily life to melt away.

Challenging Mountaineering and Climbing: Although Zermatt is an excellent destination for outdoor enthusiasts, any mountaineering or climbing activities must be approached with extreme caution and preparation. The region's high-altitude peaks and glaciers can be dangerous, so proper training, equipment, and guidance from knowledgeable local guides are essential. When embarking on these challenging activities, visitors should thoroughly research the risks, understand their own capabilities, and proceed with extreme caution.

Sustainability and Environmental Stewardship: Zermatt is dedicated to sustainable tourism and environmental preservation, setting a shining example for alpine destinations around the world. The village's car-free policy, reliance on renewable energy, and conservation efforts demonstrate its commitment to reducing the impact of visitors while protecting the region's natural resources. Visitors to Zermatt who embrace its sustainable practices can help to preserve this alpine paradise for future generations.

Whether you're looking for breathtaking natural scenery, thrilling outdoor adventures, cultural immersion, or a luxurious mountain retreat, Zermatt provides an exceptional and unforgettable experience. By adding this Swiss alpine gem to your bucket list, you'll make lasting memories and gain a deep appreciation for the beauty and wonder of the Swiss Alps.

CHAPTER 2.

GETTING TO AND AROUND ZERMATT

Transportation Options (Train, Air, Car)

Reaching the picturesque village of Zermatt is an integral part of the alpine adventure, as the journey itself offers stunning panoramic views and a glimpse into the breathtaking Swiss landscape. Whether you choose to arrive by train, plane, or automobile, Zermatt is well-connected and easily accessible from both domestic and international points of origin.

Train Travel to Zermatt

One of the most scenic and convenient ways to get to Zermatt is by train. The Matterhorn Gotthard Bahn, a narrow-gauge railway that connects the village to the nearby town of Täsch, allows visitors to easily transfer to a shuttle train for the final 5-kilometer stretch into Zermatt's car-free city center.

The train ride from Täsch to Zermatt is a true highlight, as it winds through the dramatic alpine landscape, crossing bridges and tunnels and providing breathtaking views of the surrounding peaks and glaciers. This efficient and environmentally friendly mode of transportation comes highly recommended because it allows you to sit back, relax, and fully immerse yourself in the breathtaking scenery.

Travelers can reach Zermatt by train from a number of Swiss and international destinations. Popular starting points include Zürich, Geneva, and Milan, all of which have direct or well-connected routes to Zermatt. It's worth noting that the train journey from these major hubs can take 3-4 hours, so plan accordingly and allow plenty of time for your transfer.

Air travel to Zermatt.
Zermatt can also be reached by air; the nearest airport is Zürich International Airport (ZRH), which is about 3.5 hours by train from the village. Alternatively, travelers can fly into Geneva International Airport (GVA) or Milan Malpensa Airport (MXP), both of which are approximately 2.5-3 hours away from Zermatt by train.

When you arrive at the airport, we recommend taking advantage of Switzerland's efficient rail network to get to Zermatt. The train connections from these major hubs are well-integrated, and you can easily find schedules and buy tickets ahead of time to ensure a smooth transfer.

If you're feeling daring, you can also charter a private helicopter to take you directly to Zermatt's Heliport, which is only a short walk from the village center. This luxurious option offers a truly breathtaking aerial view of the Swiss Alps and can be an exciting way to start your Zermatt adventure.

Driving to Zermatt.

Zermatt can also be reached by car, though the village itself is designated as a car-free zone. Visitors arriving by private vehicle must first park in the nearby town of Täsch before taking the shuttle train or taxi to Zermatt.

If you decide to drive, be aware of the often treacherous alpine roads and weather conditions, particularly during the winter months. It's a good idea to have your vehicle equipped with snow tires or chains, and to become acquainted with any local driving rules or restrictions. Be prepared for road closures or diversions, as the alpine environment is unpredictable.

Regardless of your mode of transportation, we always recommend purchasing your tickets or making reservations in advance, as Zermatt can be a popular destination, especially during peak travel seasons. This will help to ensure a smooth and stress-free arrival, allowing you to fully immerse yourself in the enchanting alpine setting from the moment you arrive in this charming Swiss village.

Zermatt's Car-Free Policy and Local Mobility

One of the defining features of Zermatt is its long-standing commitment to environmental preservation and sustainable tourism, as evidenced by the village's pioneering car-free policy. Implemented in the 1950s, this visionary initiative has transformed Zermatt into a true oasis of tranquility, free from the noise and pollution of private vehicles.

The Car-Free Advantage

Zermatt's car-free status distinguishes it from many other alpine destinations, providing numerous benefits that improve the overall visitor experience. Without the presence of private cars, the village's narrow streets and charming architecture can take center stage, resulting in a delightfully pedestrian-friendly atmosphere.

The absence of exhaust fumes and traffic contributes to cleaner air and a more peaceful atmosphere, allowing visitors to fully immerse themselves in the tranquil alpine setting.

Furthermore, Zermatt's car-free policy reflects the village's strong commitment to sustainable tourism and environmental conservation. By prioritizing alternative modes of transportation, Zermatt has successfully reduced its carbon footprint while maintaining the delicate balance of its mountain ecosystem. This visionary approach is consistent with the growing global demand for eco-friendly travel experiences, making Zermatt a shining example of responsible destination management.

Getting Around Zermatt.
While private vehicles are not permitted within Zermatt's village limits, the local transportation network provides a number of convenient and environmentally friendly options to help visitors navigate the area with ease.

The Matterhorn Gotthard Bahn, the same narrow-gauge railway system that transports visitors from the nearby town of Täsch, serves as the foundation of Zermatt's local mobility. This efficient train network in Zermatt provides a dependable and seamless connection between the village center, ski areas, and other major attractions. Trains run frequently, making it easy to board and disembark as needed.

For those who prefer a slower pace, Zermatt has a vast network of walking paths and hiking trails that wind through the village and into the surrounding countryside. These well-marked routes provide an enjoyable way to explore Zermatt's charming streets, historic buildings, and scenic vistas at your leisure.

Visitors with limited mobility or who prefer not to walk can benefit from Zermatt's efficient electric taxi and shuttle services. These environmentally friendly vehicles, which include electric cars, electric buses, and even electric tuk-tuks, offer door-to-door service throughout the village and to nearby destinations.

Zermatt also provides a variety of shared mobility options, such as electric bicycles and e-scooters, which can be rented at conveniently located stations throughout the village. These sustainable modes of transportation enable visitors to cover more ground while reducing their environmental impact.

It's important to note that, while Zermatt's car-free policy is a significant advantage, it does necessitate some planning and adaptation from visitors used to the convenience of private vehicles. Prior to your arrival, familiarize yourself with the local transportation options and pack light to make it easier to navigate the village's narrow streets and pedestrian zones.

By embracing Zermatt's car-free ethos and taking advantage of the efficient local mobility network, you will not only help to preserve this alpine gem, but you will also improve your overall travel experience by fully immersing yourself in the village's serene and sustainable atmosphere.

Tips for Navigating the Region

As an experienced traveler who has had the pleasure of visiting Zermatt numerous times, I've learned a thing or two about navigating this captivating alpine region with ease and efficiency. Drawing from my own personal experiences, as well as insights gleaned from the invaluable knowledge of local residents, I'm delighted to share some insider tips to help you make the most of your Zermatt adventure.

Pre-Plan your itinerary.

One of the keys to a smooth Zermatt experience is to do your research before you arrive. Take the time to research and plan your daily activities, keeping in mind the various modes of transportation, attraction hours, and any seasonal changes that may affect your schedule. This will not only help you make the best use of your time, but will also ensure that you do not miss out on any must-see sights or experiences.

Many of Zermatt's top attractions, including the Matterhorn Glacier Paradise and the Gornergrat Railway, can be extremely popular, especially during peak travel seasons. By purchasing tickets or making reservations ahead of time, you can avoid the disappointment of sold-out experiences and move through the village with a well-organized itinerary.

Leverage local knowledge.

The friendly and welcoming residents of Zermatt have a wealth of local knowledge, which is one of the most valuable assets you will have. Don't be afraid to speak with the hotel concierge, shop owners, or even other tourists; they'll often be happy to provide insider tips and recommendations tailored to your interests and travel style.

For example, the hotel staff may be able to advise you on the best times to visit Matterhorn Glacier Paradise to avoid crowds, or they may recommend hidden hiking trails that provide a more serene and authentic alpine experience. Using this local knowledge can enhance your Zermatt adventure and lead you to hidden gems that you might otherwise miss.

Pack wisely and dress for the elements.
Given Zermatt's high elevation and unpredictable mountain weather, it's critical to pack and dress appropriately. Invest in high-quality, moisture-wicking base layers, warm insulating layers, and weatherproof outerwear that will keep you safe from sudden rain, snow, or cold temperatures. Don't forget to bring sturdy, well-worn hiking boots, as the village's cobblestone streets and mountain trails can be difficult for unprepared footwear.

It's also a good idea to bring any necessary medications, high-energy snacks, and a reusable water bottle to keep you hydrated on your adventures. Remember that Zermatt is a car-free zone, so pack light and choose luggage that is easy to transport through the village's pedestrian-friendly streets.

Embrace the slow pace.
One of the most enjoyable aspects of visiting Zermatt is the opportunity to slow down and fully immerse yourself in the peaceful alpine environment. Resist the urge to rush from one

activity to the next and instead enjoy the village's relaxed pace. Take the time to enjoy a leisurely lunch, browse charming boutiques, or simply wander the picturesque streets, allowing yourself to be captivated by the region's breathtaking natural beauty.

By changing your mindset and making room for flexibility in your schedule, you'll be able to truly connect with the rhythm of Zermatt and return home feeling refreshed, rejuvenated, and full of unforgettable memories.

Explore beyond the village.
While Zermatt has many attractions and activities, don't limit your exploration to the village. Consider day trips or guided excursions to neighboring areas such as the Gorner Gorge, the Findel Glacier, or the nearby town of Täsch, which serves as the Zermatt region's transportation hub.

These surrounding areas offer opportunities to immerse yourself in the breathtaking alpine landscapes, discover lesser-known hiking trails, and gain a better understanding of the region's cultural and natural heritage. Consult with local experts or your hotel concierge to create a well-rounded itinerary that highlights the full range of the Zermatt experience.

With these insider tips and a sense of adventure, you'll be well-equipped to navigate Zermatt like a seasoned pro, ensuring that your visit to this captivating Swiss village is nothing short of unforgettable.

CHAPTER 3.

ACCOMMODATIONS IN ZERMATT

Luxury Hotels and Resorts

Zermatt is renowned for its exceptional collection of luxury hotels and resorts, each offering a unique blend of alpine elegance, impeccable service, and breathtaking views of the surrounding peaks. Whether you're seeking a pampering spa retreat or a sophisticated base for your outdoor adventures, the village's high-end accommodations are sure to impress.

Grand Hotel Zermatterhof

Located in the heart of Zermatt, the iconic Grand Hotel Zermatterhof is a true alpine hospitality icon. This 5-star hotel, which has been open since 1879, is conveniently located near the village center and the Matterhorn Glacier Paradise gondola station. Guests are greeted by the hotel's stunning neo-Baroque architecture, which includes intricate woodcarvings and a commanding tower overlooking the village.

The Grand Hotel Zermatterhof has 78 luxuriously appointed rooms and suites, all with traditional alpine decor, plush furnishings, and panoramic views of the Matterhorn or the surrounding mountains. Amenities include a large wellness center with an indoor pool, a cutting-edge fitness facility, and a variety of indulgent spa treatments. The hotel's culinary offerings are equally impressive, with several dining options serving exquisite Swiss and international cuisine.

Rates at the Grand Hotel Zermatterhof typically start at around $700 per night during the peak season, with discounts available for off-peak travel. Reservations can be made directly through the hotel's website at www.grandhotelzermatterhof.ch or by calling +41 27 966 66 00.

The Riffelalp Resort
The Riffelalp Resort, located at an altitude of 2,222 meters, is a true mountain oasis with breathtaking views of the Matterhorn and the surrounding Pennine Alps. This 5-star resort, located just a short ride on the Gornergrat railway from the village center, offers a tranquil and exclusive retreat for those looking for a luxurious alpine experience.

The Riffelalp Resort has 65 elegantly appointed rooms and suites, each with a distinct alpine-inspired design and private balconies or terraces overlooking the breathtaking views. Guests can enjoy the resort's extensive wellness facilities, which include an indoor pool, sauna, steam room, and a variety of relaxing spa treatments. The culinary offerings are equally impressive, with numerous dining establishments serving delectable Swiss and international fare.

Rates at the Riffelalp Resort typically start at around $800 per night during the peak season, with lower rates available during the shoulder seasons. Reservations can be made by visiting the resort's website at www.riffelalp.com or by calling +41 27 966 05 55.

Romantik Hotel Schweizerhof

The Romantik Hotel Schweizerhof, located in the heart of Zermatt, is a historic 5-star property that seamlessly combines traditional alpine charm and modern luxury. This family-owned hotel, which has been open since 1845, is conveniently located near the village's main square and the Matterhorn Glacier Paradise gondola station.

The Romantik Hotel Schweizerhof has 59 elegantly appointed rooms and suites, each with its own distinct character and breathtaking views of the Matterhorn or surrounding peaks. Guests can enjoy the hotel's renowned wellness facilities, which include an indoor pool, sauna, steam room, and a variety of rejuvenating spa treatments. The hotel's dining options are equally impressive, including an award-winning restaurant that serves exquisite Swiss and international fare.

Rates at the Romantik Hotel Schweizerhof typically start at around $600 per night during the peak season, with discounts available for off-peak travel. Reservations can be made by visiting the hotel's website at www.schweizerhof-zermatt.ch or by calling +41 27 966 66 00.

Mont Cervin Palace

The Mont Cervin Palace, which overlooks the iconic Matterhorn, is a luxurious 5-star hotel that provides an unforgettable alpine experience. This historic property, which first opened its doors in 1852, has been meticulously restored and modernized, striking the ideal balance of timeless elegance and contemporary comforts.

The Mont Cervin Palace has 150 spacious rooms and suites, each decorated with a mix of traditional alpine elements and modern amenities. Guests can use the hotel's extensive wellness facilities, which include an indoor pool, sauna, steam room, and full-service spa. The Mont Cervin Palace offers an equally impressive dining experience, with multiple restaurants serving exceptional Swiss and international cuisine, as well as a cozy lounge bar.

Rates at the Mont Cervin Palace typically start at around $700 per night during the peak season, with discounts available for off-peak travel. Reservations can be made by visiting the hotel's website at www.montcervinpalace.ch or by calling +41 27 966 88 88.

The Omnia

The Omnia, located on a private mountain in the heart of Zermatt, is a stunning 5-star design hotel that provides a truly unique and exclusive alpine experience. This contemporary property, designed by renowned architect Ali Tayar, boasts clean lines, natural materials, and breathtaking panoramic views of the Matterhorn and its surrounding mountains.

The Omnia's 30 rooms and suites are elegantly designed, with floor-to-ceiling windows framing the breathtaking mountain views. Guests can enjoy the hotel's extensive wellness facilities, which include an indoor pool, sauna, steam room, and a variety of relaxing spa treatments. The Omnia's dining options are equally impressive, featuring a Michelin-starred restaurant that serves exquisite Swiss and international cuisine.

Rates at The Omnia typically start at around $800 per night during the peak season, with discounts available for off-peak travel. Reservations can be made by visiting the hotel's website at www.theomnia.com or by calling +41 27 966 71 71.

With its exceptional collection of luxury hotels and resorts, Zermatt offers travelers a truly unparalleled alpine experience, blending the village's rich history and stunning natural beauty with the ultimate in comfort, service, and amenities. Whether you're seeking a pampering spa retreat or a sophisticated base for your outdoor adventures, Zermatt's high-end accommodations are sure to exceed your expectations.

Mid-Range and Budget-Friendly Stays

While Zermatt is renowned for its luxurious hotels and resorts, the village also offers a variety of more budget-friendly and mid-range accommodations that cater to a range of travel budgets and preferences. Whether you're seeking a cozy chalet, a charming guesthouse, or a simple yet comfortable hotel, Zermatt has a diverse selection of options to suit your needs.

Chalet Hotel Schönegg

The Chalet Hotel Schönegg, located just a short walk from the village center, provides a delightful blend of traditional alpine charm and modern amenities. This three-star hotel has 41 well-appointed rooms and suites, all with rustic-inspired decor, plush furnishings, and breathtaking views of the surrounding peaks.

The Chalet Hotel Schönegg offers guests an indoor pool, sauna, and fitness center, as well as an on-site restaurant serving delicious Swiss and international cuisine. The hotel also provides convenient ski storage and a shuttle service to the nearby slopes.

Rates at the Chalet Hotel Schönegg typically start at around $250 per night during the peak season, with discounts available for off-peak travel and longer stays. Reservations can be made by visiting the hotel's website at www.hotelschoenegg.ch or by calling +41 27 966 18 18.

Garni Hotel Testa Grigia

For travelers looking for a more affordable option, the Garni Hotel Testa Grigia provides cozy accommodation in a convenient location. This 3-star hotel, located just a 5-minute walk from the village center, has 28 cozy rooms and suites, each with a traditional alpine aesthetic and modern amenities.

While the Garni Hotel Testa Grigia may not have as many amenities as its luxury counterparts, it does provide guests with a comfortable base from which to explore Zermatt and the surrounding area. A shared lounge area, free Wi-Fi, and a continental breakfast are available daily.

Rates at the Garni Hotel Testa Grigia typically start at around $150 per night during the peak season, making it an excellent choice for travelers on a tighter budget. Reservations can be made by visiting the hotel's website at www.testagriglia.ch or by calling +41 27 966 44 33.

Alpenhotel Fleurs de Zermatt

The Alpenhotel Fleurs de Zermatt, located just a 10-minute walk from the Matterhorn Glacier Paradise lift station, provides a charming and affordable accommodation option for visitors to Zermatt. This 3-star hotel has 28 comfortable rooms, many of which have spectacular views of the Matterhorn or the surrounding peaks.

The Alpenhotel Fleurs de Zermatt offers a variety of amenities, including a restaurant serving Swiss and international cuisine, a lounge bar, and a sun terrace with panoramic views. The hotel also offers ski storage and a shuttle service to nearby slopes.

Rates at the Alpenhotel Fleurs de Zermatt typically start at around $200 per night during the peak season, with discounts available for longer stays and off-peak travel. Reservations can be made by visiting the hotel's website at www.fleursdezermatt.ch or by calling +41 27 966 66 24.

Backstage Boutique SPA Hotel
The Backstage Boutique SPA Hotel is a stylish and modern option for travelers looking for a one-of-a-kind and design-forward accommodation. This 4-star hotel, only a short walk from the village center, has 33 well-appointed rooms and suites with a modern alpine aesthetic and high-end amenities.

Guests at the Backstage Boutique SPA Hotel can enjoy the property's extensive wellness facilities, which include an indoor pool, sauna, steam room, and a variety of rejuvenating spa treatments. The hotel also has a trendy restaurant and bar serving delicious Swiss and international cuisine.

Rates at the Backstage Boutique SPA Hotel typically start at around $350 per night during the peak season, making it a more mid-range option compared to the village's ultra-luxury resorts. Reservations can be made by visiting the hotel's website at www.backstagezermatt.ch or by calling +41 27 966 66 00.

Whether you're traveling on a tight budget or looking for a more mid-range accommodation option, Zermatt has a variety of comfortable and well-appointed options to meet your needs. By carefully researching and selecting the right property, you can have a memorable alpine experience without breaking the bank.

Chalets, Apartments, and Unique Lodging

In addition to the range of luxury hotels and mid-range accommodations, Zermatt also offers a diverse selection of chalets, apartments, and other unique lodging options that allow visitors to immerse themselves in the village's cozy alpine ambiance and enjoy a more personalized, home-away-from-home experience.

Zermatt Luxury Chalets

Zermatt's luxury chalets are ideal for travelers looking for a more exclusive and intimate alpine escape. These beautifully appointed private residences, often situated in prime locations with stunning views of the Matterhorn, provide the ideal balance of space, privacy, and high-end amenities.

One such example is the Chalet Edelweiss, a stunning 5-bedroom chalet that can sleep up to 10 people. This opulent property, located in a secluded area just a 5-minute walk from the village center, boasts lavish interiors with rustic-chic décor, a private sauna, and a large terrace with a hot tub and panoramic mountain views. During peak season, rates at the Chalet Edelweiss start around $2,000 per night, with discounts available for longer stays.

Another popular luxury chalet option is the Chalet Zermatt Peak, a seven-bedroom residence that can accommodate up to 14 guests. This magnificent property, located high above the village, features a contemporary alpine design, an indoor swimming pool, a cinema room, and a dedicated wellness area with a sauna and massage room. During peak season, rates at the Chalet Zermatt Peak start around $3,500 per night.

Guests interested in booking a Zermatt luxury chalet can visit specialized rental platforms like www.zermattluxurychalets.com or www.chaletowners.com, or work directly with a local concierge service to find the perfect property for their needs.

Zermatt Apartments and Vacation Rentals
In addition to the village's luxury chalets, Zermatt also offers a wide range of more budget-friendly apartment and vacation rental options, ideal for families, groups, or those seeking a more independent and flexible accommodation experience.

One such example is the Apartment Matterhorn View, a modern and well-appointed two-bedroom unit that can sleep up to four people. This apartment, just a 10-minute walk from the village center, has a spacious open-plan layout, a fully equipped kitchen, and a private balcony with stunning views of the iconic Matterhorn. Rates for the Apartment Matterhorn View typically start around $250 per night.

For those looking for a more unique and authentic alpine experience, Zermatt also has a selection of traditional wooden chalets and farmhouses that have been converted into vacation rentals. One such property is Chalet Grünenwald, a beautifully restored 19th-century farmhouse that can accommodate up to ten guests. This charming chalet boasts rustic-inspired interiors, a private sauna, and a large outdoor terrace with views of the surrounding mountains. Chalet Grünenwald's rates start around $500 per night.

Guests interested in booking an apartment or vacation rental in Zermatt can explore platforms such as Airbnb, VRBO, or work directly with local rental agencies like Zermatt Vacation Rentals (www.zermattrentalcompany.com) or Engel & Völkers (www.engelvoelkers.com/en-ch/zermatt).

Unique Lodging Options
Beyond the traditional hotel and chalet accommodations, Zermatt provides a variety of more unique and unconventional lodging options for the adventurous and curious.

One such example is the Igloo Village, a seasonal attraction that lets visitors experience the magic of sleeping in a handcrafted igloo, complete with cozy sleeping bags and the soothing sounds of the nearby glacier. The Igloo Village is typically open from January to March, with rates beginning around $150 per person.

For a truly off-the-grid experience, visit the Hörnlihütte, a historic mountain hut at the base of the Matterhorn. This rustic accommodation, which is only accessible by foot or helicopter, provides a one-of-a-kind opportunity to immerse oneself in the stunning alpine environment while also connecting with the region's rich mountaineering heritage. Reservations for the Hörnlihütte are available through the Swiss Alpine Club (www.sac-cas.ch).

Whether you want the privacy and luxury of a chalet, the convenience and independence of an apartment, or the thrill of a truly unique lodging experience, Zermatt's diverse range of accommodation options ensures that there is something for everyone's preferences and budget.

CHAPTER 4.

EXPLORING THE ICONIC MATTERHORN

History and Significance of the Matterhorn

Towering majestically over the village of Zermatt, the Matterhorn is undoubtedly the crown jewel of the Swiss Alps and one of the most recognized mountain peaks in the world. This iconic, pyramidal-shaped mountain has captivated the hearts and minds of adventurers, mountaineers, and nature enthusiasts for centuries, with its sheer, towering walls and daring summit offering a true challenge to even the most experienced climbers.

The Matterhorn's history is as dramatic and captivating as the mountain itself, beginning in the early nineteenth century with the first recorded attempts to conquer its summit. Prior to this time, the mountain was largely unexplored, with treacherous slopes and harsh weather deterring all but the most daring explorers.

The Matterhorn was finally conquered by humans in 1865, when a team of climbers led by the legendary English mountaineer Edward Whymper arrived at the summit after several failed attempts. Unfortunately, the descent from the peak was marred by a disastrous accident that claimed the lives of four of Whymper's companions, cementing the Matterhorn's reputation as one of the most difficult and dangerous mountains in the world.

Despite this early tragedy, the Matterhorn's allure grew stronger over the decades that followed, as mountaineers from all over the world flocked to Zermatt to put their skills to the test on its formidable slopes. Lucy Walker made the first female ascent of the Matterhorn in 1877, cementing the mountain's reputation as a true symbol of human determination and the never-ending pursuit of personal challenge.

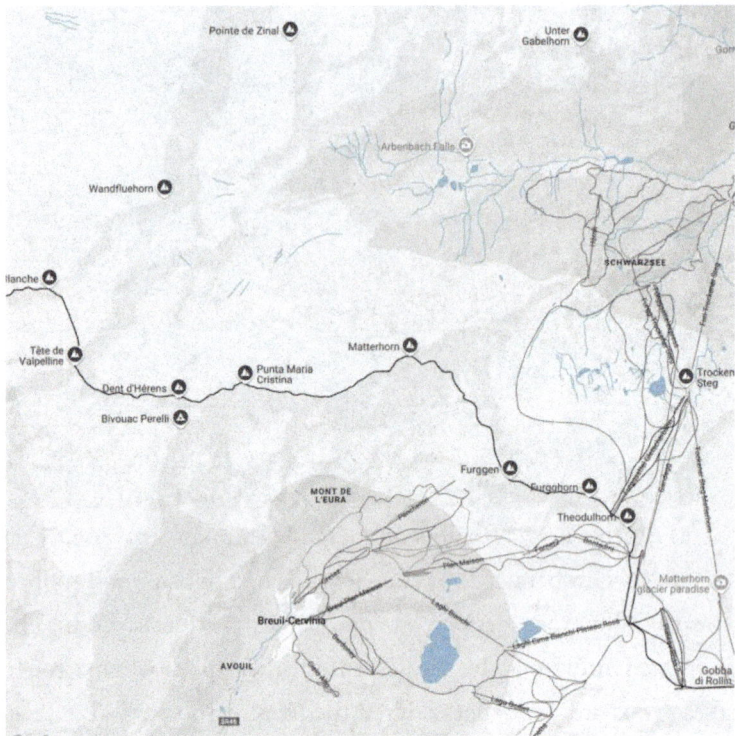

Today, the Matterhorn captivates and inspires visitors from all walks of life, demonstrating the enduring power of nature and the human spirit. Its sheer, striking walls, visible from nearly every vantage point in Zermatt, have become an instantly recognizable symbol, appearing on the labels of countless Swiss products and serving as a visual representation of the country's unparalleled alpine grandeur.

Beyond its physical presence, the Matterhorn has enormous cultural and historical significance, with its conquest marking a watershed moment in mountaineering history. The stories of the early expeditions, the triumphs and tragedies that occurred on its slopes, and the ongoing efforts to preserve and protect this natural wonder have all contributed to the Matterhorn's status as a revered and beloved symbol, not only in Zermatt and Switzerland, but all over the world.

As visitors to Zermatt, the opportunity to see the Matterhorn in all of its glory, learn about its fascinating history, and perhaps even attempt a climb or hike in its shadow is truly unforgettable. Whether you're a seasoned mountaineer or a nature lover simply wanting to be in the presence of this awe-inspiring peak, the Matterhorn will leave an indelible mark on your heart and mind, inspiring a deep appreciation for the power and beauty of the natural world.

Best Viewpoints and Observation Decks

One of the joys of visiting Zermatt is the opportunity to witness the Matterhorn from a multitude of vantage points, each offering a unique perspective on this iconic alpine peak. Whether you're seeking a sweeping, panoramic view or a close-up glimpse of the mountain's striking features, Zermatt is home to a wealth of exceptional viewing platforms and observation decks that are sure to leave a lasting impression.

Matterhorn Glacier Paradise

For the ultimate Matterhorn experience, head to the Matterhorn Glacier Paradise, the highest cable car station in Europe at an altitude of 3,883 meters (12,740 feet). From this lofty perch, visitors are treated to a truly breathtaking 360-degree view of the Matterhorn, as well as the surrounding Pennine Alps and the Gorner Glacier.

The Matterhorn Glacier Paradise complex includes a cutting-edge, glass-enclosed observation deck known as the Himmelsleiter (Stairway to Heaven), which extends out over the mountain's edge, providing a thrilling and unobstructed view. Adventurers can also visit the on-site Ice Palace, a frozen wonderland of intricate ice sculptures and tunnels, or hike the Glacier Trail to get a closer look at the mountain's glacial formations.

Reaching the Matterhorn Glacier Paradise is a must-see during any visit to Zermatt, and the journey itself is unforgettable. Guests can reach the station via a series of cable cars, each with breathtaking views as they ascend the mountain. Reservations are strongly advised, especially during the peak summer season, to guarantee your spot on this once-in-a-lifetime adventure.

Gornergrat

Another iconic Matterhorn viewpoint is the Gornergrat, a scenic railway that takes visitors to an elevation of 3,089 meters (10,135 feet) for a breathtaking panoramic view of the mountain and its surrounding glaciers. Visitors to the Gornergrat's observation deck and the adjacent Kulmhotel can enjoy a panoramic view of the Matterhorn, the Liskamm, the Dufourspitze, and countless other peaks that make up the Pennine Alps.

The journey to the Gornergrat is a true highlight, with the cogwheel railway winding its way through a breathtaking alpine landscape, revealing glimpses of the Matterhorn at each turn. Throughout the journey, passengers can disembark at various stations to explore hiking trails, visit the Gornergrat Kulmhotel, or simply enjoy the breathtaking views.

One of the Gornergrat's primary advantages is its accessibility, making it an excellent choice for visitors of all ages and fitness levels. The railway is open year-round, with the added benefit of snow-covered landscapes and the opportunity to see wildlife such as ibex and chamois.

Sunnegga

For those looking for a more intimate and less crowded Matterhorn viewing experience, the Sunnegga viewpoint is a hidden gem worth discovering. Sunnegga, which is accessible via a funicular railway from Zermatt's center, provides a unique perspective on the mountain, with its observation deck and hiking trails offering a close-up view of the Matterhorn's dramatic, rocky face.

The Sunnegga viewpoint is especially appealing to nature enthusiasts because it connects to a network of well-marked hiking trails that wind through the surrounding alpine meadows and forests. Along the way, visitors may see marmots, ibex, and a variety of bird species.

One of the primary benefits of the Sunnegga viewpoint is its relative tranquillity, especially when compared to the more crowded Matterhorn Glacier Paradise and Gornergrat stations. This makes it an excellent choice for those looking for a more peaceful and contemplative Matterhorn experience, allowing visitors to fully immerse themselves in the mountain's majestic presence.

Regardless of which viewpoint you choose, seeing the Matterhorn in all its glory is an unforgettable experience that will leave a lasting impression. Whether you're admiring the mountain from afar or getting up close, the sheer scale and grandeur of this iconic peak will leave even the most experienced traveler in awe and wonder.

Matterhorn Climbing Expeditions

For the ultimate Matterhorn experience, there is no substitute for attempting to conquer the mountain itself through a guided climbing expedition. The Matterhorn has long been regarded as one of the most challenging and thrilling mountaineering challenges in the world, attracting experienced climbers from across the globe who seek to test their skills and mettle against its imposing walls and treacherous conditions.

However, it is critical to approach a Matterhorn climbing expedition with extreme caution, planning, and respect for the mountain's harsh nature. Attempting to climb the Matterhorn without proper training, equipment, and guidance can be extremely dangerous, with the mountain's history claiming the lives of even the most experienced climbers.

Choosing the Right Climbing Operator

When it comes to Matterhorn climbing expeditions, it's critical to choose a reputable and experienced guiding company that values safety and expertise above all else. Some of the most reputable operators in Zermatt include the renowned Alpin Center Zermatt, which has been leading successful Matterhorn ascents for over 50 years, as well as Alpinschule Zermatt and Bergführer Zermatt, both of which have teams of highly skilled and certified mountain guides.

These operators not only provide technical support and equipment, but they also offer comprehensive training and preparation programs to ensure that climbers are physically and mentally prepared to face the challenges of the Matterhorn. From pre-climb conditioning exercises to detailed weather and safety briefings, these companies go to great lengths to ensure the success and safety of their expeditions.

Expedition Itineraries and Logistics

A typical Matterhorn climbing expedition with a reputable guiding company will typically last between 3 to 5 days, with the actual summit attempt taking place over the course of a single day. The expedition itinerary may include:

- Day 1: Arrival in Zermatt, gear check, and acclimatization hikes
- Day 2: Transfer to the Hörnlihütte mountain hut, final preparations, and an early start for the summit push
- Day 3: Summit attempt, with a carefully timed descent back to the Hörnlihütte
- Day 4: Descent to Zermatt, with optional visits to the Matterhorn Museum or other local attractions
- Day 5: Departure from Zermatt

Climbers will be supported by experienced guides throughout the expedition, who will handle all logistics, from transportation and lodging to summit attempt and descent coordination. This level of support is critical, as attempting to climb the Matterhorn without the supervision of experienced professionals can be extremely dangerous and ill-advised.

Preparing for the Challenge

Climbing the Matterhorn is a significant physical and mental challenge, and it's essential that aspiring mountaineers are well-prepared before attempting the expedition. This includes:
- Extensive physical training to build endurance, strength, and stamina
- Mastering essential mountaineering skills, such as rope work, ice axe techniques, and navigation
- Acquiring the necessary technical equipment, including specialized clothing, climbing harnesses, and safety gear
- Undergoing thorough medical checkups to ensure fitness and identify any potential health concerns

It's also worth noting that the Matterhorn expedition may not be suitable for everyone, so potential climbers should carefully consider their skill level, experience, and physical fitness before taking on the challenge. Reputable guiding companies will provide honest assessments and recommendations to ensure that each climber is adequately prepared to handle the expedition's demands.

A successful Matterhorn climb can be a truly transformative and deeply rewarding experience for those who are up for the challenge, allowing them to push their personal achievement limits while immersing themselves in the rich history and unparalleled beauty of this iconic alpine peak.

The Scenic Gornergrat Railway

For those seeking to experience the grandeur of the Matterhorn and the surrounding Pennine Alps without the rigors of a strenuous mountain climb, the Gornergrat Railway offers a truly exceptional and accessible alternative. This historic, cogwheel railway has been transporting visitors to the heights of the Swiss Alps since 1898, providing a breathtaking journey and unparalleled views along the way.

The Gornergrat Railway departs from the heart of Zermatt, whisking passengers on a 33-minute ascent to the Gornergrat summit station, situated at an impressive elevation of 3,089 meters (10,135 feet). Throughout the journey, the train winds its way through a stunning alpine landscape, offering glimpses of the Matterhorn and the surrounding glaciers and peaks that only add to the sense of awe and wonder.

The Journey to Gornergrat

The Gornergrat Railway experience begins in Zermatt, where passengers can purchase tickets and board the train. The cogwheel carriages, which can hold up to 125 passengers, are outfitted with panoramic windows and comfortable seating, ensuring that everyone has a clear view of the breathtaking scenery.

As the train slowly climbs the mountain, passing through a series of tunnels and bridges, the views become more breathtaking. Passengers will see views of the Gorner Glacier, the iconic

Matterhorn, and a slew of other snow-capped peaks that make up the Pennine Alps. The train makes several stops along the way, allowing passengers to disembark and explore the mountainside's numerous hiking trails and viewpoints.

One of the journey's highlights is the approach to Gornergrat summit station, where the train makes a series of steep, switchback turns, providing passengers with a thrilling and visually stunning ride to the top.

The Gornergrat Summit Experience.
When visitors arrive at the Gornergrat summit station, they are greeted by a panoramic observation deck that provides breathtaking views of the Matterhorn and the surrounding peaks. This is the ideal location to enjoy the grandeur of the Swiss Alps, take unforgettable photographs, and possibly spot some of the local wildlife, such as ibex and chamois, who call these lofty heights home.

In addition to the observation deck, the Gornergrat complex includes the Kulmhotel, a historic mountain hotel that provides comfortable lodging and dining options for those looking to extend their stay and fully immerse themselves in the alpine environment. The hotel's sun terrace and on-site restaurant are the ideal places to take in the breathtaking views and refuel after a day of exploring.

For those looking for a more active experience, the Gornergrat also has access to a network of well-marked hiking trails that wind through the surrounding alpine meadows and glaciers, providing plenty of opportunities to stretch one's legs and get up close to the region's natural wonders.

Considerations and Cautions

While the Gornergrat Railway is an immensely popular and accessible way to experience the Matterhorn and the Swiss Alps, it's important for visitors to be mindful of a few key considerations:

- The railway is open year-round, but weather can be unpredictable, especially during the winter. Prepare with appropriate clothing and equipment.
- The high-altitude environment can be difficult for some people, and they should be aware of the risk of altitude sickness. Gradual ascent and acclimatization are recommended.
- The Gornergrat summit can get crowded, especially during peak tourist seasons. Arriving early or going on off-peak days can help you avoid the biggest crowds.

By keeping these factors in mind and planning accordingly, visitors can ensure that their Gornergrat Railway experience is truly unforgettable and enriching, providing a unique and awe-inspiring view of the Matterhorn and the breathtaking natural beauty of the Swiss Alps.

CHAPTER 5.

TOP OUTDOOR ADVENTURES

World-Class Skiing and Snowboarding

For outdoor enthusiasts, Zermatt is undoubtedly one of the premier destinations in the world for skiing and snowboarding. With its extensive network of slopes, world-class lift system, and breathtaking alpine scenery, the Zermatt-Matterhorn ski area offers an unparalleled winter sports experience that attracts skiers and snowboarders from across the globe.

The Zermatt-Matterhorn Ski Area

Spanning an impressive 360 kilometers (225 miles) of groomed pistes, the Zermatt-Matterhorn ski area is one of the largest and most diverse in the Swiss Alps. Catering to a wide range of skill levels, the area features everything from gentle, beginner-friendly slopes to challenging, expert-level runs that will test the skills of even the most seasoned winter sports enthusiasts.

One of the most notable features of the Zermatt-Matterhorn ski area is its exceptional lift system, which includes cutting-edge gondolas, chairlifts, and surface tows that transport skiers and snowboarders up the mountain with ease. This efficient and user-friendly infrastructure allows visitors to spend less time waiting in lines and more time enjoying the slopes.

Another significant advantage of the Zermatt-Matterhorn ski area is the year-round snow coverage provided by the region's high-altitude glaciers. This means that the slopes are usually open from late November to early May, providing an extended winter sports season that is unparalleled in many other alpine destinations.

Who is this for?

The Zermatt-Matterhorn ski area welcomes a diverse range of winter sports enthusiasts, from families and beginners to expert shredders and freestylers. The extensive network of slopes, which includes designated learning areas, well-kept pistes, and difficult off-piste terrain, ensures that there is something for everyone.

Families and beginner skiers will find plenty of gentle, wide-open runs, as well as dedicated ski schools and equipment rental shops to help them develop their skills and confidence on the slopes. Meanwhile, more advanced skiers and snowboarders will be enthralled by the area's breathtaking high-altitude terrain, which includes a thrilling mix of steep, technical runs, expansive powder fields, and adrenaline-pumping terrain parks.

Getting Expert Help and Booking Your Adventure

To make the most of your skiing or snowboarding experience in Zermatt, consult with local experts and plan your activities ahead of time. The village is home to a diverse range of ski schools, equipment rental shops, and tour operators who can offer valuable insights, personalized instruction, and seamless logistical support.

The Snowli Ski School is one of Zermatt's most reputable and well-established ski schools, offering both group and private lessons for skiers of all skill levels. Group lessons typically cost around $70 per person per day, whereas private lessons can cost between $150 and $300 per person per day, depending on the number of participants and the level of instruction required.

For those seeking a more all-inclusive winter sports package, companies like Zermatt Alpin Center (www.zermatt-alpin.ch) and Bergbahnen Zermatt (www.matterhornparadise.ch) offer a range of lift ticket, equipment rental, and lesson combinations, with prices starting at around $100 per person, per day for a basic lift ticket and equipment rental.

It is important to note that booking your skiing or snowboarding activities in advance, especially during the peak winter season, can help ensure availability and the best rates. Many local operators provide online booking and reservation systems, making it simple to plan and secure your winter sports adventure long before you arrive in Zermatt.

Whether you're an experienced skier or a first-time snowboarder, the Zermatt-Matterhorn ski area provides an unforgettable winter sports experience that will leave a lasting impression. With world-class facilities, expert guidance, and breathtaking alpine scenery, this iconic destination is a must-see for any winter sports enthusiast.

Hiking Trails and Alpine Activities

Beyond the world-class skiing and snowboarding that Zermatt is renowned for, the village and its surrounding region also offer a wealth of exceptional hiking trails and alpine activities that cater to outdoor enthusiasts of all skill levels. From leisurely walks through picturesque meadows to challenging, high-altitude treks that put one's endurance and agility to the test, Zermatt's diverse array of hiking and alpine experiences is sure to captivate and inspire.

Zermatt's Hiking Trail Network

The Zermatt area has a vast network of well-marked and maintained hiking trails that wind through the breathtaking Pennine Alps, allowing visitors to immerse themselves in the region's stunning natural beauty. Whether you want a leisurely, family-friendly stroll or a strenuous, full-day expedition, there is a trail to suit every preference and skill level.

The **Blauherd-Fluhalp Trail** is a moderate, 6.5-kilometer (4-mile) hike that takes hikers through alpine meadows and past tranquil mountain lakes, with stunning views of the iconic Matterhorn in the background. This trail is ideal for those new to hiking or families with young children, as it features gradual ascents and well-marked signage throughout.

For more experienced hikers looking for a greater challenge, the Hörnli Ridge Trail is a must-see, offering a strenuous full-day trek to the Hörnlihütte mountain hut at the base of the Matterhorn. This 10-kilometer (6.2-mile) route, which climbs over 1,200 meters (3,940 feet), rewards hikers with breathtaking views, the opportunity to see local wildlife, and the chance to immerse themselves in the region's rich mountaineering history.

To ensure a safe and enjoyable hiking experience, visitors should consult with local guides or the Zermatt tourist office for current trail information, assess their fitness and skill level, and plan their route accordingly. Many of the region's more difficult trails require proper equipment, such as sturdy hiking boots, trekking poles, and weather-appropriate clothing.

Alpine Activities & Excursions

In addition to hiking, Zermatt and the surrounding Pennine Alps provide a variety of exhilarating alpine activities and excursions that allow visitors to fully appreciate the region's rugged, natural beauty.

For thrill-seekers, going on a guided mountaineering expedition to the summit of the Matterhorn or other nearby peaks is a once-in-a-lifetime opportunity. These challenging, multi-day expeditions, which are best completed with the assistance of expert mountain guides, provide an opportunity to push one's physical and mental limits while taking in the grandeur of the Swiss Alps.

Those looking for a less strenuous but equally breathtaking alpine adventure can take a scenic flight over the Matterhorn and its surrounding glaciers. These helicopter tours offer a unique bird's-eye view of the region's majestic landscapes, providing an unrivaled perspective that cannot be obtained from the ground.

For families and nature lovers, the Zermatt region provides numerous opportunities to observe local wildlife, such as ibex, chamois, and a variety of bird species. Guided nature walks and wildlife-spotting excursions are excellent ways to learn about the area's rich biodiversity and gain a better understanding of the fragile alpine ecosystem.

Regardless of your preferred outdoor activity, Zermatt's extensive network of hiking trails, mountaineering challenges, and alpine activities offers something to captivate and inspire visitors of all ages and skill levels. With the guidance of experienced local operators and a deep respect for the natural environment, the opportunities for adventure and exploration in this breathtaking corner of the Swiss Alps are truly limitless.

Paragliding, Mountain Biking, and More

In addition to the world-class skiing, hiking, and mountaineering opportunities that Zermatt is renowned for, the region also offers a diverse array of thrilling, adrenaline-fueled outdoor activities that allow visitors to experience the Swiss Alps from a unique and exhilarating perspective.

Paragliding

Paragliding, which takes you high above the Matterhorn and the surrounding Pennine Alps, is without a doubt one of the most breathtaking ways to experience the majesty of Zermatt's alpine landscape. This gravity-defying sport provides a smooth, silent, and remarkably gentle flight, allowing participants to glide through the air while taking in unparalleled panoramic views of the region's iconic mountain peaks, glacial valleys, and pristine alpine meadows.

For those new to paragliding, Zermatt has a number of reputable operators that offer tandem flights, in which visitors are paired with an experienced pilot who handles the technical aspects of the flight, leaving the participant to simply sit back, relax, and enjoy the breathtaking views. These tandem flights typically cost $200 to $300 per person, depending on the length and itinerary of the excursion.

More daring thrill seekers may choose to earn their wings and become certified paraglider pilots, with several local schools providing comprehensive training programs covering everything from equipment handling and launch techniques to advanced soaring and landing skills. While the initial investment in training and equipment may be more substantial, the freedom and exhilaration of piloting one's own paraglider over the Swiss Alps is truly unique.

Regardless of your skill level or experience, you must entrust your paragliding adventure to a trustworthy and safety-conscious operator. Zermatt is home to several highly regarded companies that hire only the most skilled and experienced pilots and use cutting-edge safety equipment and technology to provide an unforgettable and worry-free experience.

Mountain Biking

For those who want to explore Zermatt at a slower pace, the area's extensive network of well-maintained mountain bike trails offers an excellent opportunity to experience the alpine landscape in an adrenaline-fueled, yet completely immersive, manner.

The Zermatt-Matterhorn region is a true mountain biking hotspot, with a diverse range of trails suitable for riders of all abilities. There is something for every riding style, from gentle, family-friendly routes through picturesque meadows to technical, downhill-oriented singletrack that will challenge even the most experienced mountain bikers.

The Gornergrat Trail, a thrilling 13-kilometer (8-mile) descent from the Gornergrat summit station at an elevation of 3,089 meters (10,135 feet) to the village of Zermatt, is one of Zermatt's mountain biking highlights. This difficult but thrilling trail rewards daring cyclists with breathtaking views of the Matterhorn and the Gorner Glacier, as well as the satisfaction of completing a genuine alpine descent.

Zermatt has a number of well-equipped bike shops and tour operators that can arrange everything from high-performance rental bikes to expert-led group rides and skills clinics. Bicycle rentals typically cost between $50 and $100 per day, depending on the quality and type of bike.

As with any outdoor adventure in the Swiss Alps, proceed with caution, respect the natural environment, and wear appropriate safety equipment, such as a well-fitting helmet, sturdy gloves, and protective clothing. This allows mountain bikers to fully experience the thrill of the ride while remaining safe and enjoyable.

Other Outdoor Pursuits

In addition to paragliding and mountain biking, Zermatt and the surrounding Pennine Alps offer a wealth of other exciting outdoor activities and adventures for visitors to explore:

Rock climbing: For those looking to put their skills to the test on sheer alpine walls, Zermatt has a variety of world-class rock climbing routes ranging in difficulty from beginner to expert-level challenges.

Canyoning: The region's rugged, glacier-carved terrain is ideal for adrenaline-fueled canyoning expeditions, which take participants through cascading waterfalls, natural pools, and narrow ravines.

E-biking: With Zermatt's extensive network of e-bike-friendly trails and routes, visitors can easily access remote alpine vistas and enjoy the region's scenic splendor with little effort.

Glacier trekking: Guided tours and excursions to the Gorner and Theodul glaciers provide an unparalleled opportunity to witness the dramatic, ever-changing world of alpine ice formations up close.

Regardless of your preferred outdoor activity, Zermatt and the surrounding Pennine Alps offer numerous opportunities for adventure, exploration, and the creation of lasting memories. By taking advantage of the region's diverse range of activities and attractions, visitors can fully immerse themselves in the breathtaking natural beauty and thrilling challenges that define this iconic Swiss alpine destination.

Guided Tours and Experiences

For those seeking to make the most of their time in Zermatt and the surrounding Pennine Alps, guided tours and specialized experiences offer an unparalleled opportunity to delve deeper into the region's rich history, diverse culture, and awe-inspiring natural wonders. With the expertise and local knowledge of seasoned guides, visitors can gain a newfound appreciation for this iconic Swiss alpine destination.

Cultural and Historical Explorations

Zermatt's mountaineering roots and close ties to the Matterhorn have resulted in a rich cultural heritage that is well worth exploring. One of the best ways to do so is to take a guided tour of the Matterhorn Museum, which features captivating stories and artifacts from the mountain's illustrious history.

These guided museum tours not only educate visitors about the region's mountaineering history, but also about the Valais community's traditions and way of life. Visitors can expect to learn about the difficulties faced by early alpine explorers, the evolution of mountaineering equipment and techniques, and the Matterhorn's lasting significance in the collective imagination of the Swiss people.

For a more immersive cultural experience, consider taking a guided walking tour of Zermatt's historic village center. These tours, led by knowledgeable local guides, will take you through Zermatt's charming streets and alleyways, highlighting the distinctive architecture, local shops, and time-honored traditions that have defined the town for generations.

Culinary Explorations

No trip to Zermatt is complete without sampling the region's exceptional culinary offerings, and guided food and wine tours are an excellent way to delve into the flavors that define Swiss alpine cuisine.

These tours frequently include stops at local artisanal producers, such as cheesemakers and vintners, where guests can learn about the traditional techniques and ingredients used to make the region's famous raclette, fondue, and award-winning wines. Many tour operators also arrange for exclusive tastings and pairings, allowing participants to experience the flavors of Zermatt in a more intimate and educational setting.

For a truly one-of-a-kind dining experience, book a guided tour that includes a meal at the historic Findelhof restaurant, which has been serving traditional Valais specialties in its cozy mountainside setting for over a century. Diners can enjoy an exceptional meal while also learning about the cultural and culinary traditions that have shaped the Zermatt region from a knowledgeable host.

Nature and Adventure Experiences
Given Zermatt's reputation as a premier outdoor recreation destination, it's no surprise that the region also provides a plethora of guided nature and adventure experiences that allow visitors to explore the breathtaking alpine landscape in a safe and enriching environment.

From guided hiking and wildlife-spotting excursions to thrilling paragliding and glacier trekking tours, these specialized experiences allow you to immerse yourself in the natural wonders of the Pennine Alps while benefiting from seasoned guides' expertise and local knowledge. These professionals not only ensure their guests' safety and comfort, but also provide invaluable information about the region's unique flora, fauna, and geological features.

The Gornergrat Railway tour, which combines the traditional train journey to the Gornergrat summit with a guided exploration of the surrounding alpine environment, is a particularly memorable guided experience. This one-of-a-kind experience allows visitors to fully immerse themselves in the breathtaking scenery while learning about the historical and environmental significance of this iconic Swiss landmark.

When booking guided tours and experiences in Zermatt, it is critical to conduct research and choose reputable operators who prioritize safety, sustainability, and providing exceptional customer service. Many of the region's top-rated tour companies provide online booking and pre-trip planning services, making it simple to incorporate these enriching activities into your overall Zermatt experience.

Visitors to Zermatt can improve their understanding and appreciation of this captivating Swiss alpine destination by taking advantage of the numerous guided tour and experience options available, resulting in lasting memories and a deeper connection to the natural and cultural wonders that define this iconic region.

CHAPTER 6.

CULINARY DELIGHTS OF ZERMATT

Traditional Swiss Cuisine

Switzerland, with its stunning Alpine backdrop, is not only renowned for its breathtaking landscapes but also for its rich culinary heritage. In Zermatt, a village nestled at the foot of the iconic Matterhorn, traditional Swiss cuisine comes alive, offering a delightful blend of flavors and regional specialties.

Embrace the Fondue Tradition

One cannot discuss Swiss cuisine without mentioning fondue. This iconic dish, made by melting a combination of cheeses—usually Gruyère and Emmental—provides a communal dining experience that warms both the body and the spirit. When eating fondue, it's best to pair it with a robust white wine, like Fendant, which complements the creamy texture perfectly. For a unique twist, try a fondue made with truffles or herbs, which add aromatic depth to this classic dish.

Savor the Raclette Experience.

Raclette is another traditional Swiss dish. This dish consists of melting a wheel of raclette cheese and scraping it over boiled potatoes, pickles, and cured meats. The experience is more than just the food; it is also about the camaraderie that surrounds it. I recommend stopping by one of Zermatt's charming mountain huts for an authentic raclette experience, where the breathtaking views complement the flavor.

Indulge in Rösti

Rösti, a crispy potato dish that can be served as a side or main course, is another must-try. It originated in the German-speaking part of Switzerland and is made by grating potatoes, frying them until golden, and topping them with cheese, eggs, or smoked salmon. This dish exemplifies the simplicity and heartiness of Swiss cuisine.

Explore Local Game and Fish

Given Zermatt's alpine setting, local game such as venison, chamois, and wild boar are prominent on menus. These meats are frequently prepared with rich sauces and served with seasonal vegetables, providing a taste of the region's natural abundance. Don't miss out on fresh fish from nearby lakes, such as perch or trout, which are often elegantly prepared and served.

While eating Swiss cheese is a highlight, moderation is essential. The richness of the cheese can be overwhelming, especially when served with heavy dishes such as fondue and raclette. Balance your meal with fresh salads or light vegetable dishes to make your dining experience more enjoyable without feeling weighed down.

Sweet endings: Swiss desserts.

No culinary journey in Switzerland is complete without trying traditional desserts. Try a slice of Nusstorte, a nut-filled Engadin pastry, or Täfeli, a Swiss chocolate that melts in the mouth. For a lighter option, try **meringue** served with double cream, a classic dessert that perfectly balances sweetness and texture.

Zermatt's culinary delights capture the heart and soul of Swiss tradition. Whether you're sharing a pot of fondue with friends or savoring rösti while gazing at the Matterhorn, the flavors of this region promise to leave a lasting impression. Embrace the experience, savor every bite, and let Switzerland's culinary heritage enrich your visit.

Recommended Restaurants and Eateries in Zermatt

Zermatt is a culinary treasure trove, offering a diverse array of dining options that cater to various palates. Whether you're in the mood for traditional Swiss cuisine or international flavors, here are some of the top eateries to explore during your visit.

1. Restaurant Schäferstube
Restaurant Schäferstube, located in the heart of Zermatt, embodies the charm of Swiss tradition. The rustic wooden interior creates a cozy atmosphere, ideal for sharing hearty meals after a day of exploring.

Don't miss their signature cheese fondue, which is rich and creamy and made with local cheeses. Pair it with a glass of Fendant wine for a true Swiss experience. For something heartier, the lamb dishes stand out, particularly the slow-cooked lamb shank, which melts in your mouth. Make a reservation, especially during peak season, because this restaurant is a local favorite that fills up quickly.

2. The Omnia.

The Omnia, perched above the village, provides breathtaking views of the Matterhorn as well as a luxurious dining experience. The restaurant blends modern design with Swiss warmth, making it an excellent choice for a special occasion. The tasting menu is a must-try, featuring a delicious fusion of Swiss and international flavors. Their signature dish, "Wild Game Ravioli," is exquisite, full of flavor, and beautifully presented. Don't forget to try their decadent dessert, the chocolate fondant.

Caution The Omnia can be quite pricey, so it's worth checking the menu in advance to ensure it fits your budget.

3. Chez Vrony

Chez Vrony is a popular mountain restaurant with stunning views and a focus on local ingredients. The atmosphere is relaxed and welcoming, ideal for a casual lunch after skiing. Their homemade rösti, served with a variety of toppings such as salmon or mushrooms, is highly recommended. The venison burger is another standout, with a succulent taste of local game. Complement your meal with a refreshing local beer.

Tip: Arrive early to secure a good table on the terrace, especially during the months when the views are breathtaking.

4. Restaurant Whymper-Stube

This restaurant honors the famous mountaineer Edward Whymper, the first to summit the Matterhorn. The décor reflects a rich mountaineering history, making it an interesting place to eat. The fondue here is exceptional, made with a secret blend of cheeses that adds a unique twist. The raclette is also highly recommended and comes with a wide variety of sides. For dessert, try the homemade apple – it's a delightful way to end your meal.

Advice: The ambiance can get lively, especially during dinner service. If you prefer a quieter dining experience, consider going earlier in the evening.

5. Pizzeria Da Antonio

Pizzeria Da Antonio, a warm, family-friendly restaurant, offers authentic Italian dishes for those looking for a change from Swiss cuisine. This eatery is popular with both locals and tourists. Their wood-fired pizzas are exceptional, with a thin crust and fresh toppings. The "Quattro Stagioni" is a crowd favorite. If you're craving pasta, the homemade tagliatelle with truffle sauce is delicious.

Tip: They offer a takeaway option, so if you're in a hurry or prefer a cozy night in, this is a great choice.

6. Bergrestaurant Blatten

Bergrestaurant Blatten, located at a stunning elevation, is ideal for those looking to combine dining and breathtaking mountain views. It's an excellent location for a mid-hike meal. The grilled meats are exceptional, particularly the pork ribs, which are tender and flavorful. Their salads are also fresh and vibrant, making an excellent accompaniment to the heavier dishes.

Caution: The restaurant is only accessible via hiking trails or cable car, so plan your trip accordingly.

Zermatt's culinary scene is as diverse as its landscape, with options for everyone. From traditional Swiss favorites to international delights, each restaurant offers a distinct dining experience that reflects the alpine village's charm. Remember to make reservations whenever possible, especially during peak seasons, and be willing to try local specialties that will make your trip memorable. Enjoy your journey through Zermatt's flavors!

Swiss Wines and Other Beverages: A Taste of Zermatt

Switzerland may not be the first country that comes to mind when you think of wine, but its unique terroirs and dedicated winemakers produce exceptional wines that are well worth exploring. In Zermatt, you'll find a delightful selection of local wines and other beverages that perfectly complement the region's culinary offerings.

Swiss Wines: A Hidden Gem

1. Fendant (Chasselas)
Fendant is a white wine made with the Chasselas grape, which is primarily grown in Valais. It has a light, crisp flavor profile with

fruity and floral notes. This wine complements traditional Swiss dishes like fondue and raclette because its acidity cuts through the richness of the melted cheese. Fendant is available on the wine lists of most local restaurants, particularly those serving Swiss cuisine, such as Restaurant Schäferstube and The Omnia.

2. Pinot Noir.

Swiss Pinot Noir is valued for its quality and complexity. The cooler climate of the Valais region promotes the development of elegant flavors, which frequently include red berry notes with earthy undertones. This versatile red wine goes well with a wide range of dishes, from game meats to hearty pastas, and its subtlety makes it an excellent choice for those who value nuanced flavors. Many wine cellars in Zermatt offer Pinot Noir tastings, and it appears prominently on several restaurant menus.

3. Gamay.

While Gamay is most commonly associated with Beaujolais in France, it is also grown in Switzerland, particularly in the Geneva region. Swiss Gamay wines are typically fruity, refreshing, and easy to consume. This wine is perfect for casual dining and pairs well with lighter dishes such as salads and grilled vegetables. Its refreshing qualities make it ideal for post-ski relaxation. Look for Gamay in local wine shops or order it at bars and restaurants that specialize in regional wines.

Other Notable Beverages

1. Absinthe
Absinthe, traditionally associated with Switzerland, is a strong herbal spirit made from botanicals such as wormwood, anise, and fennel. Absinthe, also known as the "green fairy," has a complex flavor profile and is frequently served with ice water to bring out its aromatic qualities. It's an unforgettable experience that brings a touch of Swiss tradition to your evening. Many local bars in Zermatt serve absinthe, and some may even follow a traditional serving ritual for an authentic experience.

2. Swiss Beer.
Switzerland has a thriving craft beer scene, with styles ranging from lagers and ales to IPAs and stouts. Local breweries emphasize quality and traditional brewing methods. Swiss beers are frequently brewed with local ingredients, resulting in a distinct taste. They go well with hearty Swiss dishes and are an excellent way to relax after a long day on the slopes. Look for local beers at bars like The Snowboat and restaurants that serve regional cuisine.

3. Hot chocolate.

Swiss hot chocolate is a rich and decadent treat made with premium chocolate and creamy milk. After a day on the slopes, nothing beats warming up with a cup of velvety hot chocolate, often topped with whipped cream or marshmallows. Many cafés and restaurants in Zermatt, including Café 362, offer exceptional hot chocolate, which locals rave about.

Exploring Swiss wines and local beverages in Zermatt enhances your culinary experience. The menu here reflects the region's rich traditions and local flavors, with crisp whites and elegant reds, as well as unique spirits and comforting hot drinks. Accept the opportunity to sample these beverages, and let them enhance your appreciation for Zermatt's vibrant food scene!

CHAPTER 7.

ZERMATT FOR FAMILIES

Family-Friendly Attractions and Activities in Zermatt

Zermatt is a captivating Alpine destination that caters wonderfully to families traveling with children. From thrilling outdoor adventures to engaging educational experiences, this charming Swiss village offers a wealth of activities to delight visitors of all ages.

Kid-Friendly Skiing and Snowboarding

Zermatt is known for its world-class skiing, and the resort does an excellent job of accommodating families. The ski school provides excellent programs for children, with knowledgeable instructors who make learning enjoyable and safe. The Wolli Park is an excellent designated area for young children to explore the slopes, with gentle terrain and colorful, whimsical features to keep them entertained. For families with older children, the vast ski area offers an abundance of well-groomed runs catering to all skill levels, ensuring an exciting experience on the snow.

Matterhorn Glacier Paradise.

Take your family on an unforgettable journey to Europe's highest cable car station, the Matterhorn Glacier Paradise. The cutting-edge gondolas transport you to an altitude of 3,883 meters, where you can enjoy breathtaking panoramic views of the iconic Matterhorn and the surrounding glaciers. At the top, there is an observatory, a cinema, and even a restaurant where you can eat a warm meal while admiring the breathtaking views. Hiking trails allow adventurers to get up close and personal with the majestic mountainscape.

Gorner Gorge & Findel Glacier

Take a captivating tour of the Gorner Gorge, a natural wonder carved by glacial meltwater over thousands of years. The walkways and bridges along the gorge provide safe and easy access for families to explore the impressive rock formations, cascading waterfalls, and powerful rushing river. The Findel Glacier, located nearby, provides an opportunity to witness the ever-changing face of these ancient ice masses through informative displays and guided tours.

Sunnegga Fun Park

For a day of pure, unadulterated fun, visit Sunnegga Fun Park, a winter wonderland designed specifically for families. The park offers a variety of activities, such as tubing, sledding, and snow sculptures, all surrounded by breathtaking Alpine scenery. The covered magic carpet lift makes it easy for kids to get to the slopes, and there are cozy huts with hot chocolate and snacks to keep you warm.

Zermatt Folklore Museum

Immerse your family in Zermatt's rich cultural heritage by visiting the Zermatt Folklore Museum. This charming museum highlights the traditional way of life in the Swiss Alps through interactive exhibits and displays that bring history to life. Children can dress up in authentic costumes, learn about traditional crafts, and milk a virtual cow. It's an educational and entertaining experience that will leave an impression on the entire family.

Accommodations and Dining

Zermatt has a variety of family-friendly accommodations available, ranging from cozy chalets to spacious apartments with plenty of room for everyone. Many hotels and resorts cater specifically to families, offering features such as interconnecting rooms, children's play areas, and babysitting. There is a wide range of restaurants to choose from, from traditional Swiss fare to international cuisine, with many offering kid-friendly menus and options to suit even the pickiest eaters.

By taking advantage of Zermatt's many family-friendly attractions and activities, you will be able to provide your loved ones with cherished memories and an unforgettable alpine adventure. Zermatt is a hidden gem for families looking for a truly magical Swiss vacation, thanks to its exceptional facilities, breathtaking natural beauty, and warm hospitality.

Kid-Friendly Adventure Parks and Experiences

Zermatt is a destination that caters exceptionally well to families, offering a wealth of exciting and educational adventure parks and experiences tailored specifically for children. From thrilling outdoor activities to captivating indoor attractions, there is something to delight youngsters of all ages.

Sunnegga Fun Park

The Sunnegga Fun Park is a true winter wonderland that will captivate the hearts of your children. This large, family-friendly park offers a variety of snow-related activities, including tubing, sledding, and even a snow sculpture area. The covered magic carpet lift makes it easy for children to get to the slopes, and the cozy huts serving hot chocolate and snacks provide a welcome break from the cold. Caution is advised because some of the sledding runs are quite fast-paced, so close supervision is recommended, particularly for younger children.

Treetop Rope Park

For a truly thrilling experience, take your family to the Treetop Rope Park, where kids can test their skills on a series of suspended obstacles and ziplines high above the ground. The courses are designed with varying difficulty levels to ensure that both young adventurers and older daredevils can find their ideal challenge. The experienced staff provides thorough safety briefings and ensures that children are securely harnessed at all times, giving parents the confidence to let their children explore.

Matterhorn Glacier Paradise.

The Matterhorn Glacier Paradise is more than just a breathtaking view; it also provides a variety of exciting activities for families. At the top of the cable car, you'll find an observatory, a cinema, and even a restaurant where you can eat a warm meal while admiring the breathtaking views. For the daring, the hiking trails around the Matterhorn offer an opportunity to get up close and personal with the majestic mountain. Caution is advised, as the high altitude and colder temperatures may necessitate extra care for young children.

Wolli Park

The Wolli Park is an absolute gem for families with young children learning to ski or snowboard. This dedicated learning area includes gentle slopes, colorful and whimsical features, and experienced instructors who make learning enjoyable and safe. The park is specifically designed to instill confidence and skills in a safe, enjoyable environment, making it an ideal place to begin your children's winter sports journey.

Zermatt Folklore Museum

The Zermatt Folklore Museum allows you to step back in time and immerse your family in Zermatt's rich cultural heritage. This charming museum highlights the traditional way of life in the Swiss Alps through interactive exhibits and displays that bring history to life. Children can dress up in authentic costumes, learn about traditional crafts, and milk a virtual cow. It's an educational and entertaining experience that will leave an impression on the entire family.

Gorner Gorge & Findel Glacier

Take a captivating tour of the Gorner Gorge, a natural wonder carved by glacial meltwater over thousands of years. The walkways and bridges along the gorge provide safe and easy access for families to explore the impressive rock formations, cascading waterfalls, and powerful rushing river. The Findel Glacier, located nearby, provides an opportunity to witness the ever-changing face of these ancient ice masses through informative displays and guided tours. Caution is advised near the water and at the glacier, as these natural environments can be dangerous for young children.

By taking advantage of Zermatt's abundance of kid-friendly adventure parks and experiences, you can ensure that your family has long-lasting memories and an unforgettable alpine adventure. Zermatt is a true gem for families looking for a truly magical Swiss getaway, thanks to its exceptional facilities, stunning natural beauty, and a wide range of kid-friendly activities.

Tips for Traveling with Children

Zermatt is an exceptional destination for families, but traveling with children requires some special considerations. To help ensure a seamless and enjoyable experience, here are some valuable tips to keep in mind when planning your Zermatt adventure with little ones in tow.

Packing Essentials

When packing for your Zermatt trip, make sure your children's clothing is warm and weather-appropriate. Layering is essential, as the mountain climate can be quite chilly, even during the warmer months. Pack plenty of thermal underwear, fleece jackets, waterproof outerwear, and durable, insulated boots. Remember to pack essential accessories such as hats, gloves, and neck warmers to keep them warm. It's also a good idea to pack sunscreen, lip balm, and goggles or sunglasses to protect against the harsh alpine sun and glare.

Accommodations and Family Friendly Amenities

When booking your accommodations, look for hotels, resorts, or chalets that are designed specifically for families. Many properties provide amenities like interconnecting rooms, children's play areas, and babysitting services, making it easier to manage your children. Some even offer special children's menus and kid-friendly activities to keep your children entertained.

Navigating the slopes

For families with children interested in skiing or snowboarding, Zermatt's Wolli Park is a great starting point. This dedicated learning area includes gentle slopes, colorful features, and experienced instructors who make learning enjoyable and safe. Enroll your children in ski school, as the instructors are specially trained to work with children and help them gain confidence on the slopes.

Staying hydrated and fueled

Outdoor activities in the mountains can be physically demanding, so make sure your children stay hydrated and fed. Bring plenty of snacks and water bottles, and make frequent stops for warm meals or hot chocolate to replenish their energy. Many restaurants in Zermatt have kid-friendly menus and cater to family needs.

Downtime and Indoor Activities

While the outdoor adventures in Zermatt are truly captivating, it's important to plan some downtime and indoor activities to give your kids a break. The Zermatt Folklore Museum, as well as the Matterhorn Glacier Paradise's observatory and cinema, offer interesting educational experiences, while the Sunnegga Fun Park is a delightful winter wonderland full of snow-based activities.

Safety precautions

Always prioritize your children's safety when exploring Zermatt. Keep them under close supervision, especially near bodies of water or high altitudes. Ensure they are properly equipped with safety equipment, such as helmets, and adhere to all instructions and guidelines provided by activity organizers.

By following these suggestions, you can have a stress-free and memorable family vacation in the enchanting Swiss village of Zermatt. With careful planning and attention to your children's comfort and safety, you'll be able to fully immerse your family in the natural beauty, rich culture, and exciting adventures that this alpine destination has to offer.

CHAPTER 8.

PRACTICAL TRAVEL INFORMATION

Essential Packing Guide

Embarking on a journey to the enchanting Swiss village of Zermatt requires thoughtful preparation, and one of the most crucial aspects is ensuring you have the right gear and equipment. To make the most of your Zermatt adventure, it's essential to invest in a high-quality backpack that can comfortably accommodate all your essential items.

Choosing the Right Backpack

When choosing a backpack for your Zermatt trip, look for one with a strong, well-padded frame that distributes weight evenly across your back and shoulders. To ensure maximum comfort, choose a backpack with adjustable straps and a hip belt, particularly for long walks or hikes. Consider the size of the backpack based on the length of your stay and how many items you intend to bring. A backpack with a capacity of 30-40 liters is typically adequate for a week-long trip, but if you intend to do extensive hiking, you may want to consider a larger 40-50 liter pack to accommodate additional gear.

Clothing and Footwear

The alpine climate in Zermatt is unpredictable, so bring a versatile wardrobe that can adapt to changing weather conditions. Begin with a base layer of high-quality thermal underwear, both tops and bottoms, to wick moisture away and keep you warm. Mid-layers such as fleece jackets or sweaters are essential for insulation, while a waterproof and windproof outer layer, such as a breathable rain jacket and pants, will keep you safe from the elements.

Investing in a good pair of hiking boots or shoes is essential for your comfort and safety on the trail. Look for boots that provide excellent traction, ankle support, and waterproofing to keep your feet dry and stable. Break in your boots well before your trip to avoid blisters. Don't forget to bring a few pairs of high-quality hiking socks, preferably made of moisture-wicking materials such as wool or synthetic blends.

Pack a few shirts, pants, skirts, or dresses that are lightweight and breathable. Pack a warm, insulated jacket or coat for the evenings and colder days. If you plan to use the hotel's pool or spa, remember to bring a swimsuit.

Outdoor Gear & Equipment

Zermatt is an outdoor enthusiast's paradise, so make sure to pack appropriate gear for your planned activities. If you intend to hike, bring trekking poles to provide stability and relieve strain on your knees. A high-quality headlamp or flashlight is essential for navigating trails in low-light conditions, as well as for early morning or evening hikes.

For those who want to ski or snowboard, bring your boots, goggles, and gloves. If you don't own any equipment, you can rent skis, snowboards, and other gear from Zermatt's local outfitters.

If you're going to explore the Matterhorn Glacier Paradise, pack warm, weatherproof layers, such as a heavy-duty, insulated jacket and pants. A pair of gaiters can also help to keep snow and debris out of your boots.

Accessory Items

Remember to pack necessary accessories to ensure your comfort and safety. Bring a warm hat, scarf, and gloves to protect yourself from the chill. A high-quality, polarized pair of sunglasses will help reduce glare from snow and ice, while a sun hat or cap will provide extra protection from the harsh alpine sun.

Consider bringing a portable power bank to charge your electronic devices, as well as any necessary adapters or chargers. A lightweight, packable rain cover for your backpack can come in handy when it rains unexpectedly.

Don't forget to bring any necessary medications, as well as basic first-aid supplies like bandages, antiseptic wipes, and pain relievers. Hydration is essential in the mountains, so bring a reusable water bottle or hydration system.

Finally, don't forget to pack any personal items you may require, such as toiletries, a small towel, and anything else that will make you feel at ease during your Zermatt adventure.

By carefully selecting and packing the appropriate gear and equipment, you'll be well-equipped to fully immerse yourself in Zermatt's natural beauty, outdoor activities, and cultural richness. Remember to pack lightly while ensuring you have everything you need for a safe and enjoyable trip.

Additional Tips for Hikers

For those planning hiking trips in Zermatt, there are a few extra items to consider packing. A durable, weatherproof backpack cover can shield your gear from rain or snow, whereas a small rain poncho or shell can keep you dry during unexpected showers. A lightweight, packable day pack is useful for carrying essentials on day hikes, allowing you to leave your larger backpack behind.

When it comes to navigation, bring a high-quality compass and a detailed map of the nearby hiking trails. A GPS device or smartphone with a hiking app can also help you track your progress and stay on track. Don't forget to bring a portable charger to keep your electronic devices charged during your hike.

To fuel your adventures, bring a variety of energy-rich snacks like trail mix, protein bars, or dried fruit, as well as a thermos or water bottle to stay hydrated. A compact camping stove and lightweight cookware can make it easier to enjoy hot meals or beverages on longer hikes.

Finally, if you plan to go on multi-day hikes, pack a small, lightweight camping hammock or sleeping pad. This will allow you to relax and recharge in comfort as you travel through the breathtaking Zermatt landscapes.

By packing the right hiking gear, you'll be ready to take advantage of Zermatt's countless trails and breathtaking vistas, ensuring a safe and unforgettable outdoor experience.

Weather Conditions and Preparation

Nestled in the heart of the Swiss Alps, the picturesque village of Zermatt is known for its dramatic and ever-changing weather patterns. Preparing for the unique climate and environmental conditions in Zermatt is crucial to ensure a comfortable and safe visit, no matter the time of year.

Seasonal Variations
Zermatt experiences a true alpine climate, with distinct seasonal variations that can significantly impact your travel experience.

Summers are generally mild, with average temperatures ranging from 15°C (59°F) to 25°C (77°F). However, the high-altitude environment can still produce chilly, unpredictable weather, even during the warmer months.

Winters in Zermatt are notoriously cold, with average temperatures dropping below freezing and frequently reaching -10°C (14°F) or colder. Heavy snowfall is common, transforming the landscape into a winter wonderland and making conditions ideal for skiing, snowboarding, and other snow-related activities.

The shoulder seasons of spring and fall can be especially unpredictable, with a mix of sunny days and abrupt weather changes. Snowfall is not uncommon, even in late spring or early autumn, so be prepared for a variety of weather conditions.

Preparing for the elements.
Regardless of the season, it is critical to pack layers of warm, weatherproof clothing to deal with Zermatt's ever-changing conditions. Investing in high-quality thermal base layers, insulating mid-layers, and a long-lasting, waterproof outer shell will keep you comfortable and safe during your stay.

Outdoor activities like hiking or skiing require specialized equipment such as sturdy boots, gloves, and goggles. Choose fabrics that wick moisture and provide adequate insulation, as the combination of wind, precipitation, and cold temperatures can be particularly challenging.

Sunscreen and lip balm with a high SPF are required, as the harsh alpine sun can cause sunburn and windburn even on cloudy days. A good pair of polarized sunglasses will also help to reduce glare and eye strain.

Altitude Considerations

Zermatt's high elevation, with the village sitting at an average of 1,600 meters (5,250 feet) above sea level, can have an impact on your health and well-being. Some travelers, particularly those who ascend too quickly, may experience altitude sickness, which manifests as headaches, dizziness, and nausea.

To reduce the risk of altitude sickness, allow your body to gradually acclimate to the higher elevations. Spend a day or two in the village before heading up to higher elevations, such as the Matterhorn Glacier Paradise at 3,883 meters (12,740 feet). If you are concerned about altitude sickness, stay hydrated, avoid alcohol, and look into over-the-counter medications.

By becoming acquainted with Zermatt's weather patterns and preparing accordingly, you can ensure a safe, comfortable, and enjoyable stay in this breathtaking alpine destination. Packing the right gear and being aware of the high-altitude environment will allow you to fully immerse yourself in the natural beauty and outdoor activities that make Zermatt such an appealing destination.

Language, Currency, and Local Etiquette

When visiting the Swiss village of Zermatt, it's important to understand the local language, currency, and cultural etiquette to ensure a seamless and respectful experience.

Language

The primary language spoken in Zermatt is Swiss German, a distinct dialect of German. While many locals, particularly those in the tourism industry, speak English fluently, learning a few basic Swiss German phrases is always appreciated and useful.

Some useful words and phrases to know include:
- Grüezi (GROO-tsee) - Hello
- Bitte (BIT-teh) - Please
- Danke (DAHN-keh) - Thank you
- Sprechen Sie Englisch? (SHPREH-khen zee ENG-lish) - Do you speak English?
- Ich verstehe nicht (EE-h fehr-SHTAY-heh nisht) - I don't understand

Carrying a phrasebook or downloading a language-learning app can be beneficial for navigating conversations and interacting with the locals.

Currency

The Swiss franc (CHF) is the official currency in Zermatt and throughout Switzerland. It is worth noting that the Swiss franc is not affiliated with the Euro, so euros are not widely accepted in Zermatt.

When setting your budget, keep in mind that Switzerland is generally considered a more expensive destination than other European countries. Prices for lodging, food, and activities can be higher, so it's best to get a good understanding of the local costs before you go.

Most major credit cards, including Visa, MasterCard, and American Express, are widely accepted in Zermatt. However, it's still a good idea to keep some cash on hand because smaller shops, restaurants, and mountain huts may prefer cash payments.

Local Etiquette

When it comes to cultural etiquette, the Swiss are known for their punctuality, efficiency, and respect for personal space. Here are a few tips to keep in mind during your visit to Zermatt:

Be punctual: The Swiss value timeliness, so it's important to arrive at scheduled appointments or events on time.

Respect personal space: Avoid standing too close to strangers, and be mindful of personal boundaries.

Use appropriate greetings: A firm handshake is the standard greeting, and it's polite to use formal titles (e.g., Herr or Frau) when addressing people.

Avoid loud behavior: Keep your voice and conversations at a moderate volume, as the Swiss generally prefer a quieter, more reserved demeanor.

Dress appropriately: While the Swiss are generally casual, it's best to dress neatly and avoid overly casual or revealing clothing, especially in more formal settings.

Respect the environment: The Swiss are well-known for their commitment to sustainability and environmental protection, so consider your impact and adhere to local waste disposal and conservation guidelines.

Familiarizing yourself with Zermatt's language, currency, and local etiquette will allow you to navigate the destination with greater ease and respect, resulting in a more enriching and enjoyable experience.

Health, Safety, and Sustainability Tips

Ensuring the health, safety, and environmental sustainability of your Zermatt visit is a crucial aspect of planning a successful and responsible trip to this enchanting Swiss alpine destination.

Health Considerations

The high-altitude environment of Zermatt can present some unique health challenges, especially for those who are not accustomed to such elevations. Some travelers may experience altitude sickness, which includes symptoms such as headaches, nausea, and dizziness, especially if they ascend too quickly.

To reduce the risk of altitude sickness, it is recommended that you spend a day or two acclimating in the village before engaging in strenuous outdoor activities or traveling to higher elevations, such as the Matterhorn Glacier Paradise. If you're concerned about altitude sickness, stay hydrated, avoid alcohol, and consider taking over-the-counter medications.

If you have any pre-existing medical conditions or take regular medications, pack an adequate supply and consult with your doctor before your trip. It is also advisable to look up the locations of the nearest medical facilities and emergency services in Zermatt.

Safety Precautions

Zermatt's outdoor activities and alpine environment necessitate a high level of safety awareness. When participating in activities such as hiking, skiing, or snowboarding, always adhere to the guidelines and instructions provided by local guides or event organizers. Wear appropriate, well-maintained gear and equipment, and use caution on trails, slopes, and in high-altitude areas.

Be mindful of the weather and be ready to change your plans if necessary. Sudden changes in weather can make outdoor activities more dangerous, so be prepared to seek shelter or change your plans if conditions become unsafe.

It is also critical to familiarize yourself with emergency procedures and contact information in the event of an accident or incident. Keep your phone charged and accessible, and program local emergency numbers into it.

Sustainable Tourism Practices

As a responsible traveler, it is critical to practice sustainable tourism practices while visiting Zermatt. The village is dedicated to environmental conservation and has implemented a number of initiatives to reduce its carbon footprint and preserve natural resources.

When exploring Zermatt, try to minimize your environmental impact. Reduce your carbon footprint by taking public transportation, such as electric shuttle buses or the iconic Gornergrat Railway. Support local businesses and seek out accommodations that prioritize sustainability, such as those with eco-friendly certifications.

Be mindful of your waste management and make use of the recycling facilities available throughout the village. Avoid single-use plastics and bring reusable water bottles, shopping bags, and other environmentally friendly items.

To protect the fragile alpine ecosystems, stick to designated trails and paths when participating in outdoor activities. Respect the local wildlife and its habitats, and leave no trace of your presence.

During your Zermatt visit, prioritize your health, safety, and sustainable practices to help preserve this remarkable destination for future generations.

CHAPTER 9.

DAY TRIPS AND NEARBY DESTINATIONS

Discovering Surrounding Villages

While the captivating village of Zermatt is undoubtedly the main draw for many visitors to the Swiss Alps, venturing out to explore the charming neighboring communities can greatly enhance your overall experience. Each of these quaint villages has its own unique character, cultural heritage, and outdoor offerings, providing a deeper immersion into the region's stunning natural beauty and traditional way of life.

Täsch: Gateway to Zermatt

The village of Täsch, located just 5 kilometers from Zermatt, is the primary gateway for visitors to the car-free resort. When you arrive in Täsch by train or private vehicle, you will find a convenient and well-organized transportation hub that connects you to Zermatt via an efficient shuttle service.

Täsch is worth a brief visit because it provides a more peaceful alternative to Zermatt's bustling energy. Stroll through the peaceful streets, admiring traditional Swiss architecture and the Matterhorn's stunning backdrop. Consider visiting the Täsch Museum, which depicts the region's history, from its agricultural origins to the impact of tourism. For a dose of outdoor adventure, follow the hiking trails that wind through the surrounding forests and meadows, providing breathtaking views of the iconic peak.

Randa: is a picturesque mountain village.
Randa, a charming village on the Vispa River, is only a 10-minute train ride from Zermatt. A well-preserved alpine atmosphere awaits you here, complete with quaint chalets, historic buildings, and a serene ambiance that invites you to slow down and immerse yourself in the tranquility of the mountains.

Randa's main attraction is the Weisshorn, a magnificent 4,506-meter (14,783-foot) peak that towers over the village. Take a scenic hike along the Europaweg trail, which provides breathtaking views of the Weisshorn and surrounding glaciers. Along the way, you may come across traditional alpine huts serving hearty local fare and refreshing beverages.

For a more relaxed experience, go to the Randa Mineral Museum, which houses an impressive collection of fossils, minerals, and gemstones discovered in the area. After that, take a stroll through the picturesque village center, admiring the beautifully preserved wooden chalets and the historic St. Mauritius Church.

Saas-Fee: the "Pearl of the Alps"

The picturesque village of Saas-Fee, also known as the "Pearl of the Alps," is a 45-minute drive from Zermatt. Saas-Fee is surrounded by a semicircle of 4,000-meter (13,123-foot) peaks, including the majestic Dom, providing a one-of-a-kind and breathtaking mountain setting.

One of the main attractions in Saas-Fee is the Alpin Express, a cutting-edge cable car that takes you to the Mittelallalin viewpoint at an elevation of 3,457 meters (11,335 feet). From this high vantage point, you'll have panoramic views of the landscape's awe-inspiring glaciers and snow-capped peaks.

Back in the village, take a stroll through the car-free center, admiring the traditional Swiss chalets and the historic St. Nikolaus Church. Indulge in the local cuisine, which frequently includes fresh produce from the surrounding alpine meadows and dairy products from the region's well-known cheesemaking traditions.

Saas-Fee has a wide range of outdoor activities, from hiking and mountain biking in the summer to skiing and snowshoeing in the winter. Don't miss the chance to visit the Allalin Glacier, where you can admire the otherworldly ice sculptures and even have a meal or drink at the unique Ice Pavilion.

Graechen: A Stunning Hiking Destination

The charming village of Graechen, located atop a sun-drenched plateau overlooking the Matter Valley, is a popular destination for hikers and outdoor enthusiasts. Graechen, just a 30-minute drive from Zermatt, provides a peaceful respite from the crowds, with a more intimate and traditional alpine setting.

Graechen is famous for its extensive network of hiking trails that lead through lush meadows, dense forests, and past pristine mountain lakes. The Graechen Panorama Trail is an especially rewarding hike, offering breathtaking views of the Matterhorn and its surrounding peaks. Along the way, you'll come across traditional mountain huts that serve hearty local fare and refreshing drinks, making excellent pit stops to refuel while admiring the stunning scenery.

In addition to hiking, Graechen is a popular destination for mountain bikers, with a variety of routes suitable for all skill levels. Consider paragliding or hang gliding for an unforgettable experience that allows you to view the breathtaking alpine landscape from above.

Visit Graechen's charming village center, which features quaint wooden chalets, family-run shops, and inviting restaurants. Stop by the local cheese dairy to sample the region's famous dairy products, or visit the St. Mauritius Church, which dates back to the 13th century and showcases the village's rich cultural heritage.

Findeln: A picturesque Hamlet with breathtaking views.

Nestled high above Zermatt, the tiny hamlet of Findeln is a true hidden gem worth discovering during your trip to the region. Findeln, which is accessible via a scenic 45-minute hike from Zermatt or a short ride on the Sunnegga Express funicular, provides a peaceful respite from the busier main village with its cluster of traditional Swiss chalets, historic barns, and breathtaking views of Mount Matterhorn.

One of Findeln's main attractions is the Edelweiss Stübli, a quaint mountain restaurant that serves delectable local cuisine in a cozy, authentic setting. Enjoy regional specialties such as raclette, Swiss fondue, or hearty alpine soup while admiring the majestic Matterhorn towering above.

After your meal, stroll through Findeln's quaint streets, admiring the beautifully preserved wooden structures and well-kept flower gardens that contribute to the town's timeless charm. Keep an eye out for the historic Findelbach Chapel, a picturesque religious structure that has weathered the test of time in this remote alpine environment.

For the more adventurous, Findeln is an excellent starting point for a variety of hiking trails that provide breathtaking views of the surrounding peaks and glaciers. The Europawanderweg trail, which connects Findeln and Randa, is a particularly rewarding hike, offering a unique view of the Matterhorn and tranquil alpine landscapes.

Explore the Surrounding Valleys.
In addition to the charming villages that dot the landscape around Zermatt, the region boasts several picturesque valleys that are well worth exploring. These tranquil destinations provide a glimpse into traditional rural life in the Swiss Alps, complementing the more well-known attractions of Zermatt.

One such valley is the **Matter Valley**, which runs from Zermatt to the nearby town of Stalden. You'll find quaint hamlets, historic churches, and family-run farms that have been a part of local culture for generations. Follow the winding roads or hiking trails to find hidden gems like the charming village of Herbrigen, which has beautifully preserved wooden buildings and breathtaking mountain views.

Another valley to consider is the **Turtmann Valley**, which is accessible from Taesch. This remote and sparsely populated area is a haven for hikers and nature lovers, with a network of trails leading through lush alpine meadows, past crystal-clear mountain lakes, and alongside thundering waterfalls. Keep an eye out for the iconic Swiss Blacknose sheep, which graze peacefully on the valley's high-altitude pastures.

Whether you choose to visit nearby villages or explore the captivating valleys, you will gain a better understanding and appreciation for the Swiss Alps beyond the iconic Matterhorn and the bustling town of Zermatt. These hidden gems provide a more immersive and authentic experience, allowing you to fully connect with the area's natural beauty, cultural heritage, and traditional way of life.

Glacier Paradise and Mountaineer's Cemetery

Zermatt is renowned for its stunning alpine landscapes, and two of the must-visit destinations that showcase the region's natural wonders and rich history are the Matterhorn Glacier Paradise and the Mountaineer's Cemetery.

Matterhorn Glacier Paradise

Towering above Zermatt at an impressive elevation of 3,883 meters (12,740 feet), the Matterhorn Glacier Paradise is a true alpine wonderland that offers visitors an unforgettable experience. Accessible via a state-of-the-art, high-speed gondola system, the Glacier Paradise provides access to some of the most breathtaking glacial landscapes in the Swiss Alps.

When you arrive at the top station, you'll be greeted by a panoramic viewing platform that provides breathtaking views of the surrounding peaks, including the iconic Matterhorn. Take a moment to appreciate the breathtaking scenery, which features snow-capped summits and vast expanses of ice and snow, creating an otherworldly atmosphere.

For a more immersive experience, visit the Glacier Palace, which is an intricate network of tunnels and chambers carved directly into the glacier. Admire the stunning ice sculptures, crystal-clear walls, and one-of-a-kind exhibition that explains how and why these remarkable natural wonders formed and evolved. Even in the summer, the temperature inside the glacier palace can drop below freezing, so dress warmly.

If you're feeling adventurous, consider going on a guided glacier hike or snowshoe tour. These activities allow you to explore the pristine, untouched glacial surfaces, providing a unique and exciting view of the alpine landscape. However, you should only do these activities with experienced, qualified guides who can ensure your safety and provide valuable insights into the glacial ecosystem.

For those looking for a more relaxed experience, the Matterhorn Glacier Paradise also has a panoramic restaurant and lounge where you can enjoy traditional Swiss cuisine while admiring the breathtaking views. Enjoy a hot cup of Swiss hot chocolate or a glass of local wine while gazing out at the snow-capped peaks and glaciers that surround you.

Mountaineer's Cemetery

Nestled in the heart of Zermatt, the Mountaineer's Cemetery is a solemn and poignant reminder of the dangers and challenges that mountaineers have faced throughout the region's history. This sacred ground is the final resting place of many adventurers, explorers, and guides who died while pursuing their passion for the mountains.

As you walk through the serene cemetery, you'll be struck by the headstones' simplicity and reverence, each representing a life dedicated to alpine exploration and conquest. Many of the graves are adorned with mountaineering equipment, such as ice axes, carabiners, and climbing ropes, as well as personal mementos commemorating the individuals' accomplishments and interests.

The Mountaineer's Cemetery is a sacred space for the local community and the families of those who have died, so it should be approached with respect and reverence. Take some time to consider the courage, determination, and sacrifice that have shaped the history of mountaineering in the Swiss Alps.

While the Mountaineer's Cemetery may evoke a sense of melancholy, it also represents the enduring human spirit and the allure of the mountains. The legacy of those who came before inspires others to carry on the tradition of alpine exploration, pushing the limits of what is possible and striving to overcome the challenges that the mountains present.

Whether you visit the Matterhorn Glacier Paradise or the Mountaineer's Cemetery, you will gain a profound and meaningful understanding of Zermatt's and the Swiss Alps' natural and cultural histories. By respectfully engaging with these sites, you will gain a better understanding and appreciation for the region's extraordinary landscapes and the remarkable people who have shaped its legacy.

Scenic Helicopter Tours and Excursions

For the ultimate bird's-eye view of Zermatt and the surrounding Swiss Alps, a scenic helicopter tour is an unforgettable experience that should not be missed. These exhilarating excursions offer a unique perspective on the region's breathtaking landscapes, allowing you to witness the grandeur of the Matterhorn and the expansive glacial formations from a truly awe-inspiring vantage point.

Helicopter Tours and Experiences

Several reputable helicopter operators based in Zermatt and the surrounding area provide a variety of tour options to suit different interests and budgets. Whether you want a quick aerial sightseeing trip or a more extensive aerial adventure, a helicopter tour will provide you with unforgettable memories.

One of the most popular helicopter experiences is the "Matterhorn Glacier Paradise" tour, which takes you to the top of the Matterhorn Glacier Paradise at an elevation of over 3,800 meters (12,500 feet). From this high vantage point, you'll have unrivaled 360-degree views of the Matterhorn, the Gorner Glacier, and the surrounding high-alpine mountains. This tour typically lasts 20-30 minutes, giving you enough time to fully immerse yourself in the breathtaking scenery.

For those looking for a more comprehensive aerial exploration, consider booking a "Grand Tour of the Swiss Alps" or a "Glacier and Mountain Panorama" tour. These extended helicopter flights can last an hour or more, allowing you to soar over the vast expanse of the Swiss Alps, including the iconic Matterhorn, Weisshorn, Breithorn, and other breathtaking peaks and glaciers.

Insider Tips and Recommendations.
When booking your helicopter tour, ask about the availability of "doors-off" flight options, which offer an even more thrilling and unobstructed aerial experience. However, keep in mind that these open-door flights may have additional safety requirements and are not recommended for those who are afraid of heights or for young children.

To get the most out of your visit to Zermatt, book your helicopter tour early, as weather and visibility can be unpredictable, especially at higher elevations. The warmer summer months and early fall typically provide the best conditions for these aerial excursions.

When booking your helicopter tour, ask about the availability of "doors-off" flight options, which offer an even more thrilling and unobstructed aerial experience. However, keep in mind that these open-door flights may have additional safety requirements and are not recommended for those who are afraid of heights or for young children.

It's worth noting that helicopter tours can be a significant investment, with prices ranging from around 200 to 800 Swiss francs per person, depending on duration and itinerary. While the price may be higher than for other activities, the breathtaking views and once-in-a-lifetime experience make it a truly worthwhile investment for many Zermatt visitors.

Safety considerations

When booking a helicopter tour, safety should always come first. Make sure you choose a reputable and experienced operator with a track record of safe and dependable flights. All pilots should be highly trained and licensed, and helicopters should be well-maintained and outfitted with the most advanced safety features.

Before your flight, make sure to follow all safety instructions given by the helicopter crew, including the proper use of seatbelts and any other necessary safety equipment. Throughout the excursion, stay vigilant and attentive, and follow the pilot's instructions without hesitation.

It is also critical to assess your own physical and mental preparedness for the helicopter experience. If you have motion sickness, a fear of heights, or any other condition that could be exacerbated by the flight, you should proceed with caution and look into alternative sightseeing options in Zermatt.

By prioritizing safety and selecting a reputable helicopter operator, you can ensure that your aerial adventure over the Swiss Alps is a thrilling and unforgettable highlight of your Zermatt vacation.

CHAPTER 10.

RESOURCES FOR YOUR ZERMATT VISIT

Useful Contacts and Local Experts

To ensure a seamless and enriching experience during your time in Zermatt, it's valuable to have access to a network of local experts and resources that can provide invaluable information, assistance, and insider knowledge. From official tourism offices to specialized tour guides and activity providers, these contacts can help you navigate the region's offerings and make the most of your visit.

Zermatt Tourism Office
The Zermatt Tourism Office, located in the heart of the village, is your primary point of contact for all things related to visiting and exploring the area. The friendly and knowledgeable staff can provide you with a wealth of information, including:

- Up-to-date maps, brochures, and guides to help you plan your itinerary
- Recommendations for the best hiking trails, outdoor activities, and cultural attractions
- Advice on transportation options, including the use of the efficient shuttle system
- Assistance with booking accommodations, restaurants, and various excursions

- Information on upcoming events, festivals, and seasonal activities

The Zermatt Tourism Office is an invaluable resource for both first-time visitors and experienced travelers, acting as a one-stop shop for all your informational needs. Do not hesitate to stop by and take advantage of the local team's expertise to make your Zermatt experience truly memorable.

Guided Tour Operators

Consider booking a guided tour with one of the local experts to learn more about Zermatt's history, culture, and natural wonders. These specialized guides can provide unique insights and perspectives that will help you better understand and appreciate the area.

Some of the popular guided tour options include:

- Zermatt's historical and cultural walking tours highlight the village's architectural gems and the stories behind its development.
- Hiking and trekking excursions explore scenic trails and alpine landscapes, with knowledgeable guides pointing out the local flora and fauna.
- Mountaineering and glacier tours are led by experienced alpinists who can share the fascinating history and technical aspects of climbing in the Swiss Alps.
- Themed tours, such as cheese and dairy-focused experiences, provide a glimpse into the region's traditional agricultural practices.

When choosing a guided tour, make sure to research the provider's credentials, read reviews, and select an option that matches your interests and skill level. This personal touch can enhance your understanding and appreciation for Zermatt, making your visit a truly immersive and enriching experience.

Emergency Services

In the event of an emergency, it's crucial to be aware of the local emergency contacts and resources available in Zermatt. Make a note of the following numbers and keep them handy during your stay:

- Police: 117
- Fire Brigade: 118
- Ambulance: 144
- Rescue Coordination Centre: +41 27 924 53 00

These emergency services are staffed by highly trained professionals who can respond quickly and effectively to a wide range of situations, from medical emergencies to natural disasters.

Additionally, many hotels and accommodation providers in Zermatt have a direct line to emergency services, so don't hesitate to contact your lodging if you ever need assistance.

Activity and Excursion Providers

In addition to the Zermatt Tourism Office and guided tour operators, the region is home to a number of specialized activity and excursion providers who can assist you in planning and carrying out your desired activities. These local experts can help with everything from booking tickets and making reservations to ensuring your safety and providing necessary equipment.

Some of the key providers to be aware of include:

- Mountain sports outfitters provide equipment rentals and organize activities such as hiking, climbing, skiing, and snowshoeing.
- Helicopter tour companies offer breathtaking aerial sightseeing experiences over the Swiss Alps.
- Outdoor adventure operators organize activities like paragliding, hang gliding, and e-biking.
- Cultural experience providers offer workshops and demonstrations in traditional Swiss crafts and culinary traditions.

Connecting with these local experts and providers allows you to seamlessly incorporate a variety of activities and excursions into your Zermatt itinerary, ensuring a well-rounded and immersive visit to the region.

Concierge and Hotel Assistance

If you're staying at one of Zermatt's premier hotels or resorts, you can also take advantage of the concierge services and local expertise offered by these establishments. The concierge team can assist with:

- Arranging private transfers, guides, and customized tours
- Booking reservations at the best restaurants and making dining recommendations
- Coordinating any special events, celebrations, or unique experiences
- Providing insider tips and suggestions for making the most of your time in Zermatt

By leveraging your hotel's concierge's resources and connections, you can enhance your Zermatt experience and gain access to exclusive or difficult-to-find opportunities that may not be available to the general public.

Regardless of which contacts and local experts you choose to work with, the wealth of knowledge and resources available in Zermatt will undoubtedly enhance your understanding and appreciation of this captivating Swiss alpine destination.

Additional Information Sources

In addition to the local contacts and experts available in Zermatt, there are a variety of other information sources that can help you plan and enhance your visit to this Swiss alpine destination. From online resources to specialized publications, these additional sources can provide valuable insights, up-to-date information, and inspiration for your Zermatt adventure.

Online Resources

The internet is an extensive and easily accessible source of information for planning your Zermatt trip. Begin by visiting the official Zermatt Tourism website (zermatt.ch), which provides a comprehensive guide to the area, including details on attractions, activities, lodging, and transportation. The website also includes an interactive map, event calendars, and helpful trip planning tools.

In addition to the official tourism website, consider using online travel forums and review platforms like TripAdvisor and Lonely

Planet to get firsthand accounts, recommendations, and insider tips from other travelers. These resources can assist you in discovering hidden gems, understanding local customs, and making informed decisions about your itinerary.

For specific outdoor activities and adventure planning, look into specialized websites and blogs about hiking, skiing, mountain biking, and other alpine activities. These resources can provide useful information about trail conditions, equipment rentals, and guided excursions based on your preferences.

Printed publications

While digital resources are undeniably useful, there's something to be said for the tactile experience of flipping through a well-crafted travel guide or magazine. Consider purchasing a comprehensive guidebook, such as those published by Lonely Planet, Fodor's, or Frommer's, which provide detailed information on Zermatt's history, culture, attractions, and practical travel tips.

Specialized publications about the Swiss Alps and mountaineering can also be useful sources of information. Magazines such as Mountain Gazette, Alpinist, and The Alpine Journal frequently publish articles and insights about the region's natural wonders, outdoor activities, and rich climbing history.

For a more local perspective, look for regional or national Swiss travel magazines that may have special sections or features on Zermatt and the surrounding Valais canton. These publications can provide insider information and highlight lesser-known aspects of the area that may not be covered in more general travel guides.

Social Media and Influencer Content
In the digital age, social media platforms and influential content creators can be excellent sources of information and inspiration for your Zermatt trip. Follow destination-specific Instagram accounts, such as @visitzermatt, to keep up with the latest news, events, and stunning visual representations of the region.

Additionally, look for travel influencers, bloggers, and YouTubers who have documented their experiences in Zermatt. Their firsthand accounts, insider tips, and curated photography can provide you with a unique and engaging perspective on the destination, potentially revealing hidden gems or must-see experiences that you may have missed.

When using online and social media resources, consider the reliability and objectivity of the information, and cross-reference details from multiple reputable sources to ensure accuracy.

By combining the wealth of local knowledge available in Zermatt with these additional information sources, you can create a well-rounded and truly enriching experience that immerses you in the natural beauty, cultural heritage, and adventurous spirit of this Swiss alpine wonder.

Sustainable Travel and Conservation Efforts

Zermatt, a well-known alpine destination, is deeply committed to environmental conservation and sustainable tourism practices. The local community, in collaboration with various organizations and authorities, has implemented a number of initiatives aimed at reducing the impact of visitors while also preserving the region's ecological balance for future generations.

Eco-Friendly Transportation

One of Zermatt's most notable sustainable features is its car-free village center. Visitors are encouraged to leave their personal vehicles behind and take advantage of the efficient public transportation system, which includes a network of electric shuttles, electric taxis, and a comprehensive railway connection.

The use of electric vehicles not only reduces carbon emissions but also improves the village's overall tranquility and clean air. Visitors can further reduce their environmental impact by exploring Zermatt on foot, by bicycle, or by using the well-marked hiking trails that connect the various attractions and destinations.

Renewable Energy and Waste Management

Zermatt has made significant progress toward renewable energy sources and sustainable waste management practices. Many of the village's buildings, including hotels and restaurants, are powered by hydroelectric, solar, and geothermal energy, reducing the need for fossil fuels.

Furthermore, the local waste management system promotes recycling and proper waste disposal, with clearly marked collection points throughout the village. Visitors are encouraged to support these initiatives by properly sorting their waste and reducing their overall consumption during their stay.

Conservation and Environmental Stewardship.

The surrounding natural landscapes of Zermatt, including the iconic Matterhorn and expansive glaciers, are not only visually stunning but also ecologically vulnerable. Local governments and conservation organizations work hard to protect these natural wonders and encourage responsible tourism practices.

Visitors should stick to designated hiking trails, refrain from littering, and avoid disturbing the delicate alpine flora and fauna. Guided tours and educational programs are frequently available to help visitors understand the significance of maintaining the region's ecological balance and the steps being taken to protect it.

Sustainable Accommodation and Dining

Many of Zermatt's hotels, resorts, and restaurants have adopted environmentally friendly practices to align with the village's commitment to sustainability. These may include using locally sourced and organic produce, implementing energy-saving measures, and providing guests with sustainable amenities.

When choosing your lodging and dining options, look for businesses that proudly display their environmental certifications and sustainability initiatives. These businesses not only reduce their carbon footprint, but they also help the local economy and promote the preservation of the region's natural resources.

Responsible adventure activities.

Outdoor activities in Zermatt, such as hiking, mountaineering, and skiing, can all have an impact on the fragile alpine environment. To mitigate these effects, local operators and governing bodies have established guidelines and regulations to ensure responsible and sustainable practices.

Visitors who participate in these activities are encouraged to follow the rules, respect the natural environment, and use designated trails and amenities. Hiring experienced local guides or joining organized tours can also help to reduce the impact of individual exploration while ensuring the long-term preservation of Zermatt's natural landscapes.

Visitors to Zermatt can help protect the region's natural heritage and contribute to ongoing efforts to maintain the delicate balance between tourism and environmental stewardship by adopting sustainable practices and conservation efforts. During your visit, you can help to preserve the beauty and integrity of this alpine paradise for future generations by making conscious choices and acting responsibly.

Printed in Great Britain
by Amazon